"I have been waiting for this book! I know LaTan Murphy. *Courageous Women of the Bible* is her life song. With a raw and beautiful transparency, LaTan brings women in the Bible to life in a masterful and refreshing new way. I found myself on the pages of this book and in the lives of these women. A longing for Jesus to transform my fears and doubts into a shameless audacity for Him took root as I read LaTan's beautifully crafted words. Living courageously really is the heart of this book and the soul desire of its author. What a powerful read!"

—Mary Southerland, author, speaker, and cofounder of Girlfriends in God

"My longtime friend LaTan Roland Murphy's book *Courageous Women of the Bible* is a powerful message for anyone who is ready to leave fear and insecurity behind and step into a life of confidence and freedom. Reading LaTan's words is like sitting across the table from a trustworthy friend and mentor who gets you and loves you too much to let you settle for less than God's best in your life! This book will challenge, encourage, and inspire you to trust Jesus with your whole heart as you rely on His power, presence, and promises to live courageously!"

—Renee Swope, bestselling author of *A Confident Heart*

Courageous Women of the Bible

LEAVING BEHIND FEAR AND INSECURITY FOR A LIFE OF CONFIDENCE AND FREEDOM

LATAN ROLAND MURPHY

BETHANYHOUSE
a division of Baker Publishing Group
Minneapolis, Minnesota

Published by Bethany House Publishers
11400 Hampshire Avenue South
Bloomington, Minnesota 55438
www.bethanyhouse.com

Bethany House Publishers is a division of
Baker Publishing Group, Grand Rapids, Michigan

Printed in the United States of America

Library of Congress Cataloging-in-Publication Data
Names: Murphy, LaTan Roland, author.
Title: Courageous women of the Bible : leaving behind fear and insecurity for a life of confidence and freedom / LaTan Roland Murphy.
Description: Minneapolis, Minnesota : Bethany House, 2018. | Includes bibliographical references.
Identifiers: LCCN 2017037304 | ISBN 9780764230523 (trade paper : alk. paper)
Subjects: LCSH: Women in the Bible. | Courage—Biblical teaching. | Christian women—Religious life.
Classification: LCC BS575 .M855 2018 | DDC 220.9/2082—dc23
LC record available at https://lccn.loc.gov/2017037304

Cover design by Studio Gearbox

Author is represented by the Blythe Daniel Agency.

18 19 20 21 22 23 24 7 6 5 4 3 2

Always,
to my wonderful husband, Joe Murphy,
who has been my greatest source of encouragement.
Thank you for helping me courageously "go" toward
every dream of God's heart for me.
I love you with all that I am.

Contents

Introduction

> "Be strong and courageous. Do not be afraid or terrified because of them, for the Lord your God goes with you; he will never leave you nor forsake you."
>
> Deuteronomy 31:6 NIV

The first thing you need to know about me is that I am a self-proclaimed chicken, often fearful, and seldom courageous. Courage, I've discovered through the years, is something we all need, but all lack, from time to time. Courage whispers we are *enough* when fear of failure tells us otherwise. Courage gives us the desire to try. It urges us to get up when fear says sit down.

Few of us realize our need for courage until we face a daunting life situation. While fear paralyzes, courage mobilizes beyond our circumstances—like a best friend telling us we *can* keep going. We all know courage is tested most when life gets hard. Yet it comes as we *choose* to live standing strong, pressing into our faith, and it sees us through every difficult moment you and I face.

Because I needed courage, I decided to write a book that hopefully would encourage other women too—women who also need courage. That's what started this journey to find courage in the tremendous stories of the Bible that show women displaying this essential quality. There are a few things I learned about courage that I want to pass along to you for the days you need more of it.

Courage advances us into opportunities we would otherwise shrink back from and avoid.

Courage *compels* us to use gifts otherwise left on the shelf: to write the book, sing the song, stick with the diet, run the race, start a new business. Courage helps us push through to the finish line.

Every woman needs courage because it transcends every circumstance of our busy, jam-packed lives. And it comes as we faithfully face our unknowns. Courage answers with grit when questions born of insecurity invade: Will I get the job? And if I do, will I be good at it? Am I capable of being a good wife, even though I had no strong role models to teach me how? Will I beat cancer? Will I, always the outcast, ever fit in? When our minds are overloaded with information and our hearts overwhelmed by fear, courage comes to the rescue, overcoming anxiety about our children's futures, our own futures, fear of aging, financial hardships, and even death.

The women of the Bible teach us by example how to courageously live, love, and face life victoriously. We need God's women to teach us how to keep going, particularly when the men in our lives fail to lead. It is women like the widow with two coins who encourage me to courageously give—beyond my resources—and prove God is able. And I need women like the woman with the issue of blood to teach me how to bravely come to Jesus when I feel most unclean or rejected.

As a young girl, I had no idea how much I would need Jesus and all He faithfully provides. In choosing Him, I literally chose *courage*. As He lovingly nudged my heart to come to Him, I experienced my first taste of the beautiful courage He offers those who trust His omnipotent power. Since that warm summer night, a few things have become very clear.

Courage comes as we point our feet toward the path leading to obedient living.

When life's circumstances have overwhelmed me—presenting me with unexpected or stressful changes beyond my control—my knees have buckled, many times over. In times like these, I'm grateful for courageous women who surrounded me, lifted me up, and pointed me in the right direction when I didn't know what to say, how to respond, or how to pray. Sometimes, I still feel like the little girl who fell to her knees weeping into the sawdust at a children's camp in Georgia—hot tears gushing from my eight-year-old green eyes. Although I could not see Jesus, I felt His love drawing me—magnetically giving me courage to keep walking—down the long aisle toward the altar to receive him.

My faith walk has not been perfect. But His courage goes with me down messy, sawdust pathways still today. Courage comes as I intentionally remember His faithfulness in times past—how He faithfully provided courage to make it through the teenage years, to leave home, go far away to college in Nashville, Tennessee, and step out on my own into adulthood.

His love grows sweeter and His strength more necessary as I remember how He provided courage to "fight" for a beautiful marriage of nearly thirty-four years now, courage to give birth to three miracles, courage to raise kind children in an unkind world, courage to help me grieve as cancer ravaged my brother's body and Parkinson's disease paralyzed my father. I clung to this courage when my sweet nineteen-year-old niece was tragically killed in a car crash, when my twenty-eight-year-old nephew died unexpectedly from a heart attack, and another precious nephew died, just this year, in a motorcycle accident. In times like these, although there is nothing I can do physically to change the circumstances, I am comforted knowing I am never without help. Christ, my courage-giver, fills me with hope for brighter tomorrows.

Courage enables us to have a victorious spirit when we feel like crawling into a hole. Courage moves us emotionally beyond the circumstance, over the obstacle, and pulls us out of the pits we fall into. Courage helps us to look up when we want to look down and away. Courage says keep your eyes on the goal of better days ahead.

These days, Jesus is giving me courage to grow old—to look in the mirror, see my wrinkles, and choose to be alive with wonder. And yes, it is possible to be alive with wonder all the days of your life.

We need courage every day to stick to our "no" when our precious little ones flash puppy-dog eyes of cuteness—knowing our ultimate goal is to develop godly character in the lives of our children. We need courage to hold strong in discipline—knowing the fruits of our relationships must come later.

It takes courage to run a household and juggle a career simultaneously—courage to say no to the wrong things and yes to the right things. Some of us need courage to break an addictive habit, or break off an engagement to the wrong person before it's too late.

Perhaps we've lost our self-worth and need courage to stop following the crowd.

We desperately need courage to face our messy lives. If you could see the mess in my life, you'd understand my need of courage. My life is wonderfully overwhelming, probably much like yours. I am a small-business owner, a speaker, writer, teacher, wife, mother of three, grandmother of two, sister to five, daughter-in-law, aunt to eighteen nieces and nephews, and daughter to my elderly mother. Because people matter, I put a lot of pressure on myself. A balanced life seems impossible because I simply cannot lay certain things aside. I don't have the courage I often need. But, friend, I have good news for us:

When we cannot do it all perfectly, we can do all that we do courageously.

Courage helps us to be the best we can be—in each given role God appoints us, knowing that we are doing all things for God—not to please people. Do you feel the pressure lifting from your shoulders, friend? I do! It takes courage to "let go" of our Wonder Woman mentality and rest in knowing that although we are imperfect people, we serve a perfect God who is pleased when we dedicate all that we do to Him alone. Oh, how we need sweet courage to let us know it's *okay* to fail. Courage helps us keep things in perspective when our perfectionism distorts God's reality. How we need courage to grab us by the nape of our neck, forcing us back to our feet when we want to sit down, give up, surrender in defeat to the voices telling us that if we can't do it *all* perfectly then we shouldn't try at all. This is a lie! Don't believe it!

As we draw wisdom from past mistakes, we can make courageous future choices.

God wants to use your story as He used many courageous women of the Bible to fulfill His higher purposes. When you are most tempted to throw your hands up in defeat, give up completely, turn back to a smooth-surfaced path, you can choose to keep walking it out. Courage makes the right choice, acts the right way, says the best thing, chooses the best attitude, and takes the high road. Courage admits the wrong, making us transparent and authentic. Courage never gives up on us. Courage chooses integrity instead of compromise.

Perhaps you feel the least courageous of all as you read this. I know that feeling. So let me assure you that you are in good company. Friend, may we be wise enough to step out, finding courage along the way together.

Here we go!

In this book, we will look at eleven courageous women of the Bible who were flesh and blood, like you and me. Yet they were warriors, messengers, courageous leaders—wise enough to follow God's best leading. Each woman left behind a sawdust trail of courage for us to follow. May we wisely learn from these courageous women of old, then practice being courageous women each day.

Because there are so many amazing women of the Bible, it was no easy task to pick my top eleven courageous women. But I think the ones I did choose are great role models for us. Their stories inspire and challenge us to find courage in the face of defeat and unchangeable circumstances.

Let me start by reiterating that what labels a woman as "courageous" hasn't changed since the beginning of time. But the worldly definition of courage is far different than the biblical one. Worldly courage often masks a rebellious, sinful nature. Worldly courage screams, "You can't make me do anything I don't want to do!" or "It will be my way!" Or even, "You can't stop me!"

Godly courage is mobilized by an obedient spirit—knowing the power of God is greater than the circumstances we face.

Courage by God's standards is the ability to act, regardless of human fear or frailty, and enables us to do supernatural things because we are not acting alone—God is with us. And sometimes, godly courage is manifested in the ability to not act outwardly, but to wait, pray, and be still in God's presence. To linger, listen, seek His best way to live. Real godly courage is laced with an attitude of obedient gratitude, knowing that He is able to lead, guide, and direct our lives. We can enter into a sweet place of rest knowing we can count on God to reveal how we are to live courageously in each and every moment of our lives.

Courageous behavior comes as we realize we are living for a higher cause, greater good, and better story that is being written across our beautifully imperfect lives.

In each chapter I have taken some creative license to position us emotionally inside each woman's unique life circumstances and look at how courage was manifested. But I have really tried to stay true to Scripture. Hopefully you will see a bit of yourself in each of these eleven women, or perhaps think of someone you know who has been a courageous woman in your life. I pray you will be inspired by how they each found courage.

We need to trust the reliability of Scripture when life gets messy and our hearts are facing the unknowns. I pray you will find relief in knowing there's no need to *pretend* to be tough or fearless to be counted among the courageous women of the ages. We are on a journey to leave behind fear and insecurity for a life of confidence and freedom. We will go courageously, hand in hand with the Courage-Giver.

Our lineup of courageous women includes:

- **Deborah**—Wife, judge, and ruler of Israel. Courage is needed to lead our families and others.
- **The Woman with an Issue of Blood**—Physically sick woman. Courage is needed when facing rejection.
- **The Widow with Two Coins**—Poor widow. Courage is needed to give generously in our financial hardships.
- **Jael**—Wife, warrior, divided household, decisive and courageous. Courage is needed to seize opportunities—using what's in our hands in the midst of obstacles.
- **Abigail**—Faithful wife to a selfish, foolish man. Courage is needed to do the right thing, even when your spouse or others do not.
- **Bathsheba**—Exposed bathing beauty caught in a web of sin. Courage is needed when we've acted in sin, were abused, molested, or feel violated.
- **The Samaritan Woman**—Person with a troubled past of multiple marriages. Courage is needed to simply believe there is redemption and to tell others what Christ has done for us.
- **Mary, Mother of Jesus**—Young mother. Courage is needed to have a baby, especially in unpredictable times. Mary delivered the Son of God amidst great odds and pressure around her, and we are bearers of life in uncertain times.
- **The Shulammite Woman**—Hopeless romantic. Courage is needed to express our physical love, knowing the marriage bed is undefiled.
- **Jochebed**—Mother of Moses. Courage is needed as we surrender our children and the people we care about to God.

- **The Shunammite Woman**—Hospitable wife. Courage is needed to show hospitality, taking an others-minded approach to life by welcoming others into our private lives, even when our prayers are unanswered.

I am so excited to offer you the opportunity to think about your own life and how each of these courageous women can help you to grow. At the end of each chapter you will find several questions for study and personal reflection that can be used on your own, in a small group, or in Bible study settings. As you answer each question in this *Courage Quest* segment, I hope you will linger, taking time to really think about how each woman's challenges and her responses to them help you in your own life experiences.

Another important feature of this book is a journal section, *Courage Coming—Journal Your Way to Courageous Living*. I can tell you firsthand, it's in times of quiet introspection I am able to hear God's voice most clearly. It's my sincere hope you will intentionally position yourself above the noise of life so that you can fully celebrate and evaluate how you've grown, and how you've found a bit of yourself in the lives of these incredible women of the Bible. Courage will come as you pen your fears and insecurities and how these affect your ability to live confidently and courageously free. It doesn't matter how you choose to use this journaling experience—whether you complete the corresponding journal page immediately after you finish each chapter or wait until you have read the entire book. Are you willing to join me?

A willing spirit is what courage demands—nothing more, and nothing less.

Do you feel your journey demands more than you can give? Do you desperately need courage? As you read about the eleven courageous women in this book, I pray you will invite the Almighty to join you in every part of your path, and that each relationship and situation you find yourself in will be faithfully transformed. I believe God wants to use women like you and me to do great things for *His* glory.

May we courageously leave behind fear and insecurity for a life of confidence and freedom. Let's begin by settling in underneath the palm of Deborah—the tree from which Deborah ruled and judged. I challenge you to view your life from God's higher perspective. You are, as Deborah was, the best person for your individual God-appointed job.

Nothing is allowed into our lives without God sifting it through His powerful fingers first. Will you allow Him room to prepare your heart and mind to be strong and courageous? I wish you courage for each and every day. The women in this courageous lineup have much to teach us about putting our faith into action. May we become modern-day women of courage—kingdom forces to be reckoned with!

Your courage-seeking friend,

La'lan

1

Man Up and Lead!

I doubt that Deborah, a spunky woman from Ephraim, saw herself as more than Lappidoth's wife and a prophetess before being appointed as judge and ruler, with all of Israel under her wise jurisdiction. It's doubtful Deborah ever imagined herself in such a highly appointed position as deliverer and executive leader of Israel. And I doubt that any of us can imagine all *we* are capable of with God's perfect positioning in *our* lives. But in the same way Deborah courageously stepped up to lead as the fourth judge of Israel—the only woman to have held that important position—we also can bravely step forward into the God-filled, purposed positioning of our lives.

But sometimes we fail to recognize all that we are capable of, until we are in a position demanding "more" of us. And sometimes more is required of us because others fail to do their part in a given situation. For Deborah, this occurred when Barak, a military leader appointed by God to lead the Israelite nation into battle, fearfully pulled back from his leadership role, refusing to go into battle unless Deborah accompanied him. Deborah was put in a position demanding that she add "warrior" to her already impressive résumé as judge and ruler. Too bad Barak missed his opportunity to lead strongly and faithfully, but Judge Deborah would not miss hers.

So, what's a woman to do when her world falls apart? When those she thought she could count on to fight for her greater good shrink back in fear? Scripture offers us a glimpse of Judge Deborah's world crumbling before her very eyes, and nothing could ready her for it except courage:

> And the people of Israel again did what was evil in the sight of the Lord after Ehud died. And the Lord sold them into the hand of Jabin king of Canaan, who reigned in Hazor. The commander of his army was Sisera, who lived in Harosheth-hagoyim. Then the people of Israel cried out to the Lord for help, for he had 900 chariots of iron and he oppressed the people of Israel cruelly for twenty years. Now Deborah, a prophetess, the wife of Lappidoth, was judging Israel at that time. She used to sit under the palm of Deborah between Ramah and Bethel in the hill country of Ephraim, and the people of Israel came up to her for judgment.
>
> Judges 4:1–5

Can you see her in your mind? Sitting under the palm tree, shoulders squared, jaw fixed, assessing the situations and circumstances all around with eyes of steel? Dedicating herself to the purposed positioning of God as the sun peeked through the clouds at the start of each new day? We'd be smart to do the same—seek God at the start of our day. How else could Deborah have found wisdom to lead and to fulfill each role of her life with such excellence? How can we?

As the cries of the Israelite nation traveled like the wind across the beautiful hill country of Ephraim reaching the obedient ears of Deborah, she must have struggled with her own human nature warring against her godly best. Watching the suffering and cruel oppression of the people of God and desperately wanting to experience freedom. I think that as Deborah settled under the palm tree, her mind also settled on the realization of all she'd been entrusted with. Leadership is needed in every arena of life. A country without a leader suffers. The most powerful leader is one who understands that his or her ability to lead is no match for God's leadership.

There must have been times when Deborah felt like she was hanging on by her fingernails, as the weight of her burdened heart pressed in. Did she sigh a long, disillusioned sigh—wondering what happened to the godly warriors who once fought for their nation's freedom? Did she silently whisper a prayer, her heart crying out for answers, as we do, while watching Fox News or CNN? It's hard *not* to become disillusioned with so many negative news reports.

Sometimes, while watching the news, my heart is overwhelmed and I think to myself: If I see or hear *one more* sad or bad thing, I am going to fall into total despair: rapes, murders, burglaries, terrorist attacks, Amber Alerts, sex trafficking—to name a few. How about you, friend? Do you feel the same? If so, we can sympathize with Judge Deborah's need for courage as she watched the progressive evil in *her* world. Stunned, as we are, to see how far from God's truth her world had gone.

It Takes Courage for Real Women to Face Real Enemies

Deborah was a real woman, like you and me, with real-life struggles, insecurities, and fears; yet as she devoted both her strengths and her weaknesses to God, He equipped her to listen, speak, and act with power, purpose, and anointing—in an ancient world where women rarely were leaders, and were not respected as such. Perhaps God positioned Deborah to prepare future generations of women and girls to find respect in life and leadership also. We can be inspired by Deborah, knowing that as the Israelite nation cried out to God for freedom once again, Deborah cried out to God for real-life answers to her very real-life situations.

How she must have wished the nation of Israel had remembered Joshua's words and passed them down to the next generation:

> "Only be strong and very courageous, being careful to do according to all the law that Moses my servant commanded you. Do not turn from it to the right hand or to the left, that you may have good success wherever you go. This Book of the Law shall not depart from your mouth, but you shall meditate on it day and night, so that you may be careful to do according to all that is written in it. For then you will make your way prosperous, and then you will have good success. Have I not commanded you? Be strong and courageous. Do not be frightened, and do not be dismayed, for the Lord your God is with you wherever you go."
>
> Joshua 1:7–9

Thankfully, Deborah had remained strong and courageous. God's supernatural power was with Deborah; her success as a woman was nothing short of living proof of God's loving hand on her life and leadership. Moses, Joshua, and Ehud had "manned up" to lead God's people out of bondage in times past, and now Deborah faced forward to the battle ahead—keeping the courageous legacy of others close to her heart while *creating* a godly legacy of her own for the next generation. And as she did, she courageously chose to leave behind her fears and insecurities to pursue a life of confidence and freedom.

What about you, friend? Do you have a few fears and insecurities fighting against your daily freedom? Does your enemy have a name? Deborah's enemy had a name—Sisera. And his nine hundred iron chariots were intimidating and fierce, causing panic to ripple through the band of worn-out Israelites who were surely weary from the battles they'd already faced. But God had spoken, whispering in Deborah's ear a battle plan that included a man named Barak:

> She sent and summoned Barak the son of Abinoam from Kedesh-naphtali and said to him, "Has not the Lord, the God of Israel, commanded you, 'Go, gather your men at Mount Tabor, taking 10,000 from the people of Naphtali and the people of Zebulun. And I will draw out Sisera, the general of Jabin's army, to meet you by the river Kishon with his chariots and his troops, and I will give him into your hand'?" Barak said to her, "If you will go with me, I will go, but if you will not go with me, I will not go."
>
> Judges 4:6–8

"You'll go . . . if I go with you?" Deborah must have been speechless. God had provided 10,000 people and Barak refused to go without *one woman*—Deborah. We might wonder: *Where's your courage, Barak?* Maybe we need to ask ourselves the same question: Where is our courage? Are we willing to lead courageously, or do we need someone to go with us because we lack confidence?

Barak's focus had turned away from God and toward his fears; he was looking to others for courage. I think God wants us to stop being disillusioned by the enemy, to set our prayer hearts into motion so we can live courageously, trusting that His power is *all* the power we will ever need—today, tomorrow, and forever—for every battle we will ever face.

Imagine the long line of compromisers—disgruntled, needy people waiting to hear a word of wisdom from *one* woman,

Deborah, the representative of God symbolizing peaceful living, if there was any to be found in their fallen culture. Like Barak, they also must have sensed the power residing inside of the judge and warrior Deborah. Both men and women coming with respect and expectation as Deborah sat judging and ruling over the nation of God's chosen people.[1] As her tired eyes shifted, left and then right, assessing every situation, do you think she ever grew faint because of her overwhelming responsibilities resolving issues such as land disputes or marital discord?

Our best attempt to relate to Deborah might fail. But let's think of our worst day of dealing with grumbling co-workers and aging parents, or try to relate to Deborah's exhaustion after listening to *your* family complaining about a single meal. Do you fall apart? Fall into bed feeling like a failure because your kids have been obstinate all day long and your husband is withdrawn? Now try to imagine ruling over an entire nation of grumbling adults. *That* would put most of us six feet under!

God can give us spiritual eyes to see our problems as spiritual battles that are being waged. And we can live confidently, knowing that whatever battles are yet ahead, God will equip us and provide people to support us when we need it.

> "Certainly, I will go with you," said Deborah. "But because of the course you are taking, the honor will not be yours, for the Lord will deliver Sisera into the hands of a woman." So Deborah went with Barak to Kedesh. There Barak summoned Zebulon and Naphtali, and ten thousand men went up under his command. Deborah also went up with him.
>
> Judges 4:9–10 NIV

We think our daily stress is bad? Imagine being told that Sisera's nine hundred iron chariots are coming to attack you—right in your neighborhood! It would be equivalent to nine hundred army tanks coming your way. Intimidating, huh? Remember, the Israelite nation was weary from battles past, and after battling against so many enemies, no wonder they lacked courage. As you battle against deep insecurities, do you give up or remain faithful to God—doing what you can to ensure this season of life is your most powerful one yet, with or without a man to lead you? Will you be the woman God planned for you to be? With God by your side, who needs 10,000 warriors to fight for you?

It was God going with Deborah, equipping her with the ability to persevere and to discern what she needed to say to instruct even the most powerful men in her day. Impressive, huh? It'd be like presiding over a meeting in a boardroom and having the final say. Can you see the determination in her face, her eyes filled with grace but also strength when she said to Barak, "Has not the Lord, the God of Israel, commanded you—go?"[2]

Imagine the courage it must have taken for Deborah to not only advise Barak but to go with him and the warriors into battle. I don't know about you, but I'm a princess who wants to be rescued and would rather stay in the safety of my home while my man led in battle to protect me. But I have also witnessed the strength of many military women, who would gladly have gone into battle, leading confidently because of their commitment to our country, even if they felt moments of weakness or fear.

Courage Helps Us Face Our Tomorrows

I believe that Deborah didn't always feel the strength that others thought came effortlessly for her. But obstacles are simply opportunities with God by our side—even when God's appointed man refuses to man up and lead. Deborah inspires us to "go" courageously into battle and shows us how not to squander a moment of our God-given appointments. As she exercised her faith in God, I think she became more than a number, more than just a woman. Because heaven takes note of our willingness to serve the Lord. God saw Deborah's dedicated heart and gifted her with all she would need to accomplish all that *He* desired. Nothing can stop this kind of faith gone courage, not in Deborah's life, not in your life, and not in mine:

> And Deborah said to Barak, "Up! For this is the day in which the Lord has given Sisera into your hand. Does not the Lord go out before you?"
>
> Judges 4:14

Victory demands that we get up. Lying around won't get us to our better tomorrows, friend. It takes wild courage to fight against oppression and depression. We are more than conquerors as mothers, wives, grandmothers, sisters, friends, co-workers.[3] We can lead strong, knowing that "If God is for us, who can be against us?" (Romans 8:31 NIV).

Come as you are, friend. Deborah's role as judge was symbolic and a "welcome" sign of sorts—inviting the people to come just as they were. She would stand in the gap for them, representing their individual case to God. Deborah lived before Christ's birth, when people counted on priests, judges, then kings to lead, represent, and help them through daily struggles—resolving conflicts of life and offering wisdom for living. Only the high priest could enter the sacred place where God's spirit dwelt, and that happened behind a veil.

Deborah's open-air courtroom, the palm of Deborah, provided a place where the voice of God could be heard through a judge, wife, and warrior to the people she so loved. The truth of her life-giving wisdom must have poured over the exhausted, sinful nation of Israel like pure spring water replenishing their souls. Deborah's open-air courtroom was a foreshadowing of the freedom we can experience in coming into the presence of Jesus any time, day or night; Jesus gave His life on the cross and now stands between the Father and us these precious days representing our "case"—our every life circumstance—with forgiveness, love, and grace.

Years ago, my daughter went through a very hurtful time in her life when a man who had promised to love and cherish her broke his promise. I experienced so much anger and was unable to forgive and unable to pray. My child's life had been affected, and the war raging inside of me was overwhelming. If I'd been living in Deborah's day, I might have angrily huffed and puffed my way to the palm tree where she sat judging the nation. But I am privileged, as you are, my friend, to come openly to God when I've lost my way. And sitting in my fuzzy pink bathrobe, I cried out to God, confessing my sin of bitterness, saying, *Lord, I'm so angry! I have no grace!* As hot tears poured down my grief-stricken face, I poured out my rage onto the middle of the kitchen floor. And was amazed to find the Holy Spirit met me there as I came openly, holding nothing back. I experienced a sweet spiritual epiphany as Jesus whispered, "*I am grace when you cannot extend grace; I am forgiveness when you cannot forgive. I stand in the gap between you and a holy God—representing your case, I'll do the thing you cannot do. I will fight for you. Stay near me. . . .*"[4]

Thankfully, as I chose to stay near to God, He went into battle against an enemy named anger that felt like nine hundred iron chariots wanting to turn me into a bitter woman. I am thankful for Jesus, the One who opened the way for me to come—the crazed mess that I was—into the presence of a holy God. He is the only weapon needed.

Hopefully, this puts into perspective the power of Deborah's open-air courtroom. Today, nothing can block our path leading to the gift of God's grace, mercy, and love. Come freely, friend. Come angry, bitter, and grumbling—like the unfaithful remnant of the Israelite nation, and like me—a crazed, unforgiving, courage-seeking, weeping, angry woman in a pink fuzzy bathrobe. When we are most broken, God's light will shine through all the cracks, helping us see the things others would overlook, and lighting the way for others with less courage.

It was God's light shining through Deborah that made Barak look to her for courage to go into battle. But God doesn't play favorites, friend. He wants to use each of us, His children, to lead strongly and faithfully. By dedicating our fears and insecurities to God we can discern right and wrong, good and bad, knowing when to act, like Deborah did. In wisdom, Deborah acted courageously, knowing that if Barak didn't strike in a timely manner the entire nation would be at a disadvantage and lives would be lost.

And had chicken me not acted courageously and in a timely manner on the day a copperhead snake slithered its way up the sidewalk leading to my friend's home, her family would have been at a disadvantage. Standing in my high heels and dress, I (Barak) wanted someone else—anyone else—to take care of the enemy for me. But when my friend wimped out, courage stepped in, as it had for a woman named Deborah, helping *me* to realize all that was at risk, overshadowing the fear and anxiety.

With a shovel in hand, I pressed through the fear, killing the snake and possibly saving the lives of people and pets. As with Deborah, there was no time to waste, even though I wasn't dressed to kill a snake, had never dreamed I'd be called upon to kill a snake, and hadn't had time to practice or study *Snake-Killin' for Fraidycats*. Someone had to act. Otherwise the enemy (snake) could hide in the shrubs and ambush someone later. Like Deborah, I had no one to delegate my responsibilities to, and so I dedicated my fears to God and called to Him for help—openly—without shrinking back.

I cannot express the courage God's son, Jesus, gives. Knowing that He represents us to the Father and that His Holy Spirit sets us apart helps us overcome fears and moves our hearts to engage by faith when we would normally run from difficult circumstances.

Has your enemy filled you with fear, causing you to perceive others as being set apart with power while you have been put on the shelf? No matter how unprepared or ill-equipped you feel, there's no one more capable than a woman who dedicates herself fully to God and then willingly acts when courage demands her to. The snakes on the sidewalk of your life might be temptations you are facing with fear. Are you willing to act in the moments of fear when life presents opportunities for courage to shine?

We can come seeking answers openly—as we drive down the road, our unseen power source, Jesus, right beside us. Or, we can openly seek His wise counsel while doing dishes or scrubbing the toilets. Will you allow His power to equip you for the moments demanding big courage, whether facing an enemy on the sidewalks of your life—wearing high heels, like me—or when facing the internal battles of your mind? Come to Him in prayer anywhere, any time of day, with hopes, dreams, and fears in hand—holding nothing back. Jesus' death on the cross opened the way for this kind of sweet personal intimacy with God.

Will you boldly step out to lead whatever your Israelite nation looks like? Whatever you are facing, friend, don't compromise your faith just because the other way seems easier. Courage comes when we are about to lose our footing but muster the fight to keep standing strong. God equips us with spiritual eyes to help us discern truth from lies.

Is God directing you to lead by example? Perhaps, like Deborah, you can help someone who lacks courage to do the right thing. Perhaps your strong support is what's needed for them to rise to their purposed position. One woman's courageous actions moved the next generation to faithful living. And we can lead the next generation of girls to be strong and courageous too. What could change if we gave the world God has entrusted us with something to admire and aspire to be?

> "Apart from me you can do nothing."
>
> John 15:5 NIV

We can't accomplish a lot *without* the Lord, but *with* His help we can accomplish things of lasting value. Deborah's dedication had lasting value for the nation of Israel.

Are you willing to dedicate yourself to God as Deborah did? Don't allow fear and insecurities to talk you out of acting courageously in everyday moments. Instead of filling our lives with good things, let's fill our lives with the things of lasting value. Instead of looking for our purpose in life, let's view God *as our purpose*. With God as our purpose, we can let go of the worry and live in true freedom, knowing He will help us bear fruit in our mothering, our job, and in the lives of others we influence.

Courage Sometimes Calls Us to the Lonely Path

Leading is sometimes a lonely path. The times we feel most alone are proof of God's loving desire to have us acknowledge that He is the *only* one who can fill our gaping, empty voids. Though others pulled away from their appointments, dedicated Deborah remained true to hers. Has God assigned you to a season of fighting a battle seemingly all alone? If so, don't give up. Rise, like Deborah—tenaciously, faithfully. Dedicate yourself to all that *He is* and lead others with all that *you are*. When your boss is difficult, the ministry you are leading feels fruitless, when you aren't sure where God is calling you. Don't give up—until God says. All of heaven is fighting for you—a great cloud of witnesses are cheering you to keep going and not lose the courage it has taken to get this far.[5]

I wonder if Deborah felt relieved knowing God had chosen Barak to lead the battle against Sisera? Try to remember a time in your life when so many people needed you for so many things. Remember how difficult it was to get above the noise? When my children were little I felt exhausted by the end of the day. When friends or family gave me a break, I was thrilled. Do you think Deborah imagined such a rest? To have Barak fighting *for* her and for the nation God loved? But that is not how the story went. Barak refused to go into battle *without her.*

And perhaps that is how your story has gone? Sadly, it's how my friend Amber's story went too.

Amber loved her husband, David, and believed in his leadership ability; but she was weary of telling him and expecting him to be the spiritual leader of her home. Like Barak, David was too busy fighting internal battles of his own to man up and lead in his God-given appointment to fight the spiritual battles for his family, and Amber worried his lack of interest in the things of God might affect her children's faith. But Amber courageously dedicated herself to prayer—her wisest battle plan yet. Her voice might not influence or sway her husband toward God and away from the world, but she dedicated herself to staying near to God anyway.

And God faithfully stayed near to Amber—healing the anger, resentment, and confusion. Soon Amber felt stronger in her ability to fight the enemy on the sidewalk. And she found wisdom and rest knowing God would speak truth into David's heart. She *was not* responsible for his choices. David, like the Israelites who came to the palm tree of Deborah ready for change, had to own his unwise actions and seek God for change. To continue in the same cycle of sin would be as destructive as the Israelite nation never learning from its past mistakes. Just like the Israelites found rest and peace at the feet of wise Deborah, we can find rest, peace, courage, and strength at the feet of Jesus. This is *our best battle plan* and the only plan with any hope of victory in our own lives.

When every single angle you have tried is met with a dead end, know that *you*, yourself, are an overcomer with God as the voice of wisdom. God wants you to experience life and freedom—to experience all that *He is*. Even when others are not receptive to God's call for *them*, you—one dedicated woman, with a Deborah-like courageous spirit fueled by an Almighty power—will break bondages and find true freedom.

God was Deborah's solution, and Amber's solution. Will you allow Him to be *your* solution? He is the final answer to life's big, fearful questions. And He can offer answers when confusion enslaves you.

It was under the outstretched branches of the tree of Deborah that the Israelite nation found courage to change. And it's under the strong and capable outstretched arms of Jesus that we become confident and free. Go with God, stay near to Him. He will faithfully guide when men fail to man up and lead. And He will deliver the battle into one capable woman's hands—yours!

> "If my people, who are called by my name, will humble themselves and pray and seek my face and turn from their wicked ways, then I will hear from heaven, and I will forgive their sin and will heal their land."
>
> 2 Chronicles 7:14 NIV

Stay tuned for the rest of the story of this battle—and another courageous woman's role in it—in chapter 4, "What's in Your Hand?"

COURAGE QUEST

1. Read Judges 4.
2. Do you see Deborah's need for courage? Are you able to see a bit of yourself in Deborah? Have you ever experienced a time in your life when you were called to lead but felt ill equipped to do so?
3. Think about the many roles you play. Write them down and ask God to bless each appointed position He has entrusted to you. Ask Him to help you let go of any self-appointed position that is causing added stress to your life.
4. Have you ever been forced to lead because someone else failed to do so? Surrender your hurt to God so that the next season of your life can be your most powerful.
5. How does Deborah's life encourage you to live more courageously?

2

Messy Courage

The weak and lifeless woman must have moved slowly through the crowd. Yet audaciously she pressed on, forcing one foot in front of the other, holding fast to the one thought she could focus fully on: *If only I can touch the hem of His garment—Jesus, the great healer.* Every other thought must have seemed scrambled, muted. Her physical ailment had taken a toll on her outward appearance, and her mental capacities too. How could it not? She had been bleeding for twelve long years and had suffered a great deal under the care of many doctors. To make things worse, she had spent all she had. Yet instead of getting better she grew worse.[1] When she heard about Jesus, she knew she had to come to Him. It would require big courage because she was considered "unclean." But no matter how weak, no matter how self-conscious she might have been, there was one thought driving her—compelling her to come and making the focus of what she desired crystal clear: healing.

> She came up behind him in the crowd and touched his cloak, because she thought, "If I just touch his clothes, I will be healed."
>
> Mark 5:27–28 NIV

Imagine twelve long years of suffering physically and most likely emotionally. Imagine twelve long years of isolation from society—a wretched nightmare for us social butterflies. Thankfully, desperation turned to courage—just before she lost all hope—pushing her beyond what she thought herself capable of. Like a best friend cheering her on, courage refueled her with supernatural strength to go to Jesus, regardless of the risk of someone touching her in her unclean state.

Was it the sunlight blurring her vision, or His radiance? With squinted eyes, courageously pressing through she came. Did radiant beams surround Him and engulf her weary soul—magnetically drawing her? Did her heart pound to the rhythm of her steps, fear and hope driving her, knowing this was her last resort? She'd heard rumors of how Jesus had raised the dead and set those captive free. She'd heard rumors of how He'd healed the blind and raised the sick from death to life. His name was etched into her being.

The noisy cries of the people in need of a touch could not stop her. Even Jairus, a ruler of the synagogue raising his voice above the others and pleading with Jesus to come and heal his daughter before it was too late, could not stop her.[2] Regardless of cultural reasons and the glaring eyes reminding her of her public disgrace, she came. Courage compelled her to go, and fear crumbled at the Savior's feet as perfect love enveloped her, wrapping around her fragile body like an invisible, comforting afghan. Thankfulness welled inside her as she realized she'd made it this far. With shaky, outstretched hands, she reached through the mob of strangers until, at last, her frail but eager fingers touched the hem of His garment—the Courage-Giver himself, Jesus Christ, Son of the Living God.

> Jesus turned and saw her. "Take heart, daughter," he said, "your faith has healed you." And the woman was healed at that moment.
>
> Matthew 9:22 NIV

As the rushing warmth of healing power flowed from Him, reaching deep into the core of her being, she instantly felt strong and able, abundant life filling her from the inside out. She felt alive, vibrant, and joyful. The pain she had carried in her body for so long was finally gone. Jesus had sent forth His word and healed her—completely—absorbing her affliction into himself, making it His own.[3] Did she skip, dance, run for joy, sing a song of praise—like a child free and innocent—feeling lighthearted and whole? If I'd experienced such an amazing miracle, I think I would have. What about you?

Friend, each of us is intricately designed by God—both metaphysically and physically; so our bodies and our minds respond to things differently. But most of us can sympathize with our courageous sister, having also experienced a monthly period. During this time of the month, many women experience sickness or pain, and some have feelings of falling short and being rejected if we aren't bearing children. Some of us are tearful and feel emotionally unsteady because of hormones raging during this time of the month. Many of us can remember a time when we overreacted to things we would normally let roll off our back. Even if we are well past the age of menstruation, some of us remember it being like an unwanted guest, afflicting our bodies with more than headaches and cramping. Sometimes we feel bloated, ugly, and unclean, and we don't want to be around people.

In Jesus' day, a woman in this condition was considered a social outcast. Touching her made one unclean.

> "When a woman has her regular flow of blood, the impurity of her monthly period will last seven days, and anyone who touches her will be unclean till evening."[4]
>
> Leviticus 15:19 NIV

Freedom must have felt amazing after being imprisoned by conditions beyond her control. Learning about what it was like for a woman in Jesus' day to experience this type of ostracization brings up a question for us. How much do we rely on our physical condition to define when we can come to Jesus? When life is going great we tend to forget our need for a Savior. But when we face a physical illness or someone we love is facing a painful situation, then we realize our need for Jesus, the healer. When people grow weary of hearing of our afflictions, Jesus doesn't. Be relentless in your coming, friend.

It's so important to be aware of what is happening in our body, our mind, and our soul—always. With good reason, our emotions can be all over the place. But all we have to do is consistently come to Him with our weakness and our unclean selves and He meets us with a healing of our hearts that no one else provides.

Outcast No More!

Like the woman with the issue of blood, some of us know what it feels like to be a social outcast—trying to fit into groups where the superior attitudes create walls that divide and seem to invade us with an I'm-better-than-you mentality. But we've already learned from Deborah that it takes courage to believe God will receive us just as we are without having to make ourselves "better" first. So, my question to you is: Will you come—audaciously pushing past the naysayers, the grumblers, and the complainers—and humbly lay your messy life at the feet of Jesus?

When we hit desperate times, nothing will hold us back from approaching Him—not even our pride. I'm sure if we'd been bleeding for twelve long years, we would have come screaming to Jesus, saying to others along the journey:

"Get out of my way, and don't mess with me."

"What are you looking at?"

"Oh . . . So sorry for your loss, Jairus. But while it might be too late for your daughter, it's not too late for me!"

Can you relate? We want what we want, right? And often we don't let others stand in the way of our getting what we'd like. But what is this like when it comes to our wanting Jesus? I must admit that I don't often have the same desperation for Him as I do for a perfectly organized and decorated house or an outfit that reflects how "put together" I am. Sometimes I fail to recognize my need because I've grown comfortable with my bleeding heart and run to friends for comfort and healing before going to Jesus. What about you?

But our friends and our family members can sometimes fuel the frustrations within us. It's so important to pray and seek God's face in every situation and to align our hearts with faithful friends and trustworthy, mature-minded family members who will stand with us, point us to truth, and pray for us when our physical circumstances skew our thinking. Our goal is to become courageous women who leave behind fear and intimidation for a life of confidence and freedom. Choose wisely your confidants, friend. Ask yourself who is leading whom?

I am privileged to have women share their stories with me as I travel and speak. Many candidly share about how their hormones each month lead them to think and believe. It is amazing to think that we can change who we are and our emotions based on how we feel physically. At some point in your life you've no doubt experienced this. Some women are filled with such rage and believe they are justified in the way they treat others. The woman with the issue of blood might have *felt* like throwing a hissy fit along the way, but she remained focused on Jesus and *acted* based on her need. She is a great example for us, reminding us that our circumstances don't have to rule our lives, attitudes, or actions.

What about you? Do you allow the afflictions of life to control your demeanor? Does everyone around you pay the price? Pure grit enables self-restraint. Sometimes we are too weak and too desperate to waste unnecessary energy. I think the woman coming to Jesus was looking ahead to what her life *could be*, not what it had been. We can exercise the same beautiful humility—living focused, relentless—pressing our lives into Jesus' healing power.

I realize my own need to come to Jesus with the places of my heart that need to look forward, not backward—as messy as my life may be. Do you feel your life is too messy to come to Jesus? Are there areas of your life that feel unclean? Let me encourage you that you are not alone. We all have things that we would rather clean up before we come to Him. But notice in the Scriptures how the woman with the issue of blood came anyway. She didn't allow anything to hold her back. I love that!

True confession: On an average day, I care way too much about how I look or how others perceive me. The woman with the issue of blood was not hindered by the jeering looks or words of the crowd. Instead, desperation for something bigger than herself kept her heart focused forward on one person: God personified, her help, her healer.

Determination is needed for us to move forward in life when our circumstances have held us hostage for so long. In quiet whispers, we may come to Him, escaping the mad world around us, determined to escape the crazy lives we live. A wise pastor challenged the crowd during a service I attended years ago: "When you get to the end of yourself, you will realize your need for God and come."[5] We find true rest and release when we finally realize we cannot fix the broken, messy, undone situations of life and understand our need for our powerful God.

The Bible tells us the woman had suffered a great deal under the care of many doctors and had spent all she had. Yet instead of getting better she grew worse.[6] "When she heard about Jesus, she came up behind him in the crowd and touched his cloak, because she thought, *'If I just touch his clothes, I will be healed.' Immediately her bleeding stopped and she felt in her body that she was freed from her suffering*" (Mark 5:27–29 NIV, emphasis added).

Courage gives us just enough fuel to push through the barriers, to keep our heart fixed on a goal—an end result that will be far better than our current conditions. This woman understood that after twelve long years she had the power to change her circumstances; no longer would she allow her current messy life to dictate her future living. Courage gave her the strength, and faith led her to the feet of Jesus. Jesus offered transforming power. The same power is available for every condition of our lives. If we truly believe Jesus is Lord, we have a supernatural power source available to us.

> At once Jesus realized that power had gone out from him. He turned around in the crowd and asked, *"Who touched my clothes?"*
>
> Mark 5:30 NIV, emphasis added

She knelt in her most humble, messy condition at the feet of Jesus, and her suffering paled in comparison to the joy she was about to experience. Her need had kept her going, every miserable step of the journey, while courage kept her from turning back and compelled her to draw near, to touch the dirty hem of the Savior's garment—against all the odds that she faced along the way. Every time the odds are against us, Jesus—the courage-giver—is for us!

Humility Requires Courage

Ever notice how many excuses we can make in a week's time? Women are the masters of finding excuses—gripping tightly our long lists of reasons why we can't talk to Jesus with our bleeding hearts and sin-sick souls. Somehow, we know that if we draw closer to Jesus, we will be changed. Our messes are like home to us and we feel comfortable in our old messy ways of doing life. Part of us wants to come to Jesus. But part of us enjoys being comfortable—keeping Him at a safe distance. Perhaps we kind of enjoy the pity others offer us and we fear that if we come to Jesus things will drastically change. It takes courage to admit we need "tissues for our issues," which range from being bitter and angry to physically hurting and emotionally broken. It takes courage to bring our everyday, simple, unavoidable challenges to the Savior. But it was Jesus who said, "Come to me, all you who are weary and burdened, and I will give you rest." (Matthew 11:28 NIV)

I have been so weary some days that I hardly feel like I can come to Him. But then I realize, what are my other options? And do any of those provide life like Jesus does?

Courage says, "*I will go toward Jesus instead of away from Him because my messy life needs Him. I need healing for* _______________." We can think of many things to insert, can't we?

So where does this hit you right now?

Jesus' love compels us to courageously come—just as we are:

Come Unclean

Come Cast Out

Come Forbidden

Come Forsaken

Come Forgotten

Come Rejected

Come Abused

Come Defiled

I focus on the word *come* because that is exactly what the woman with the issue of blood did. She came. Her coming released transforming power from the hem of a dirty garment worn by the Son of God.

Will you fall at the feet of Jesus today, at least in your heart? A better life is just one step away, friend. It might take some pushing and shoving, and it might be costly. But keep your eyes on Jesus, push through the crowded emotions of your life today, and simply come.

Come with hormones raging and short fuses. Come to Him to find that He will take on all that the world wants to topple you with. Let go of your strength to find His. This is where we are the safest and most fulfilled.

Could it be that Jesus wanted the crowd to see *who* it was who touched Him? To make a point that He came to save the sick, the outcast, the unclean—all who would courageously come near? For all who are forced to live in the margins of life, whether because of insecurities, cultural demands, or by choice? His blood draws us from the cross and heals our bleeding, wounded souls, heals us of the hurtful words spoken over us, gossip, paranoia, depression, physical ailments. Jesus chose to suffer and die for every contaminated, dirty thing warring against our opportunity for courageous living.

Heads turned, eyes shifted, silence fell across the crowd. There were so many pushing and shoving their way toward Him. The disciples said,

> "You see the people crowding against you," his disciples answered, "and yet you can ask, 'Who touched me?'" But Jesus kept looking around to see who had done it. Then the woman, knowing what had happened to her, came and fell at his feet and, trembling with fear, told him the whole truth. He said to her, "Daughter, your faith has healed you. Go in peace and be freed from your suffering."
>
> Mark 5:33–34 NIV

Can we even imagine how our lives would be transformed if we could "go in peace," as Jesus has overcome our suffering as well? What if we were to take our eyes off what others are saying and fix our gaze on Jesus? Instead we look for power to flow our way, not from the hem of His garment, but from

Our Jobs
Our Paycheck
Recognition
Social Media Numbers
Opinions of Others

And when we get to the end of ourselves, realizing we can't do life alone, we slowly begin to make our way through our crowded lives until at last we fall at His feet acknowledging we need Him. Sometimes we come limping along. Other times we come crawling because life has beaten us up so much we have no strength to stand. And often shame hinders our coming at all.

But regardless of when we come, or the condition we are in when we arrive, Jesus lovingly takes note of our posture toward Him. The accuser calls us a spectacle. Jesus calls us

His child. If we will quiet our souls and rise above the noise of our messy lives, we will hear Him lovingly whisper upon our arrival, "Who touched me?" Then He will gently lift us to our feet, saying, "Daughter, your faith has healed you. Go in peace. Be free from your suffering."

Have you, like the woman with the issue of blood, experienced the power of Jesus? Or are you still waiting for it—either because it's too hard to give up the load you are carrying or because you aren't sure He's interested in you? It takes courage to believe God is at work even when life seems hard.

Anne Graham Lotz challenges us with a few thoughts in line with my own, in her book *Just Give Me Jesus*:

> Could it be God has given you a platform of suffering from which you can be a witness of His power and grace to those who are watching? Because if we always feel good and look good and lead a good life,
>
> If our kids always behave
> And our boss is always pleased
> And our home is always orderly
> And our friends are always available
> And our bank account is always sufficient
> And our car always starts
> And our bodies always feel good
> If we are always patient, and kind, and thoughtful and happy and loving, others shrug because they're capable of being that way too.[7]

The conditions of our lives change year after year. One minute everything is going great. The next we find ourselves full of fear, standing on an invisible platform of hardship and suffering. But our testimony becomes tangible and powerful when our problems press us—like the woman with the issue of blood—toward the solution: Jesus, our courage. We can be strong and kind, wise and confident women of the Word. This is a by-product of our coming, our reaching, our touching the hem of Jesus' garment.

Not that we are perfect people, but transparent people. Exposing the fake, phony, and fluffy stuff. Only when we stop pretending, only when we bring our messy lives can we see the healing power of Christ. The world needs to see by example how one woman can courageously act and react with godly character, even in times of suffering.

It makes me wonder how many in the crowd of onlookers realized their personal need for Jesus as they witnessed the woman with the issue of blood transformed from weak and lifeless to alive and free. As she rose to her feet, suddenly she became the central focal point of *His* platform. Her platform was no longer the focus—He was! It isn't about others seeing us; it's about seeing Him, with 20/20 heart-and-soul vision. Although the crowd probably despised her for being there, they saw—clearly—courage personified.

I feel confident in saying we all have felt the pain of rejection at some point in our lives. We've all experienced criticism by people we thought had it all together. But some of us have been downright blessed to have never known the pain of being a social outcast.

Some of us would have to confess that our worst experience of rejection was in elementary school when the popular kids ganged up on us, barred the playground equipment like they owned it, and turned their backs as a visible sign of alienation. Your experience of rejection may run much deeper, with the physical or emotional slamming of doors on your heart as you were growing up. Whatever your history, your feelings matter to Jesus. What I really want us to take away from this story is that Jesus heals us: emotionally, physically, and spiritually. Quite simply, He loves you, sees you, and longs for you to come to Him, with no conditions barring your path.

Perhaps you've endured gut-wrenching life experiences that have left you feeling alone and isolated. If my precious mother-in-law were alive today, she would understand how you feel. For sixteen long years, cancer ravaged her beautiful body, even after multiple surgeries and chemotherapy treatments—no healing came. How could she face affliction so courageously? How was she able to become more others-minded than ever before and push through crowded, fear-filled uncertainty? How could a dying woman joyously celebrate her friends on *their* last day of treatment, *their* good news of remission? The same Jesus the woman with the issue of blood had approached helped my mother-in-law muster the strength to stand on tiptoes in the doorway of the chemo treatment room, a candlelit cupcake in hand, celebrating milestone victories of others with every fiber of her being. And neither her weakened body, her bald head, nor her hollowed eyes could diminish her courageous, loving spirit. What beautiful, messy courage on display.

Your affliction is different than an issue of blood or my mother-in-law's cancer. Do you suffer from depression, diabetes, a speech impediment that hinders your ability to communicate with confidence—leaving you feeling like a social outcast? Or perhaps it's fear of rejection, the feeling that you can't equal those around you, a bleeding heart that gushes emotional pain from the wounds of a broken marriage relationship? Perhaps you are simply sin-sick, in need of a Savior yet too weak and too discouraged to come to Him. Your afflictions might have caused you to lose hope and put you in a corner, telling you no one would want you around. It takes courage to square our shoulders, keep our head up, to shuffle through our crowded emotions and reach toward transforming power that changes, renews, and makes us whole.

Intimidation cannot stop us. Fear cannot hinder or block us. Get ready to be transformed. Can you see Him through your crowded life? If you are like me, you might have to push away from technology to catch a glimpse of the Great Healer. Peek around the heads of others blocking your view, friend. Allow yourself to be exposed, vulnerable, and humble. In doing this, you will have positioned yourself for greater things to come. Own your tomorrows by making your way to Jesus today!

COURAGE QUEST

1. Read Mark 5:25–28. Now put yourself in the sandals of the woman with the issue of blood. How do you relate to her need for messy courage?
2. Think about a time when you felt like an outcast. It's hard to want to socialize when we feel "less than" in any way. Imagine how twelve years of bleeding would make you feel. What hinders your coming to Jesus?
3. Sometimes our lives are too noisy, too cluttered, and our minds are on overload by the messiness of living. What keeps you from reaching out to Jesus, in faith, for your better tomorrow?
4. The woman was desperate for change. How about you? Is there a circumstance (physical, relational, spiritual) that you have lived with for days, weeks, months, or years and want desperately to be set free from?
5. The woman with the issue of blood was healed because of her faith and persistence in not allowing anything to keep her from Jesus. What have you learned from this courageous lady that will make your life better?

3

Courage Comes in the Most Unlikely and Least Affluent

Can you see her in your mind? The widow woman reaching deep into the pockets of her worn tunic, her arthritic fingers scooping two coins into her eager palms? Poverty might have been her lot in life, but her joy was in giving. She was only one of the many worshipers gathered from all around Israel bringing tithes and offerings to God—two copper coins, which make a penny.

I can imagine the courage in her step and gratitude in her heart, compelling her to go—to give all she had. No criticism from the Pharisees, who had rebuked the disciples for hailing Jesus as Messiah and even questioned His authority, would stop her.[1]

Quietly, she came. But everything about her coming cried out praises to her God. How could she not go? How could she not give, with so much love for her Lord? And who would notice an old widow woman anyway?

Jesus would. Jesus notices *every* woman—including you:

> And he sat opposite the treasury and watched the people putting money into the offering box. Many rich people put in large sums. And a poor widow came and put in two small copper coins, which make a penny. And he called his disciples to him and said to them, "Truly, I say to you, this poor widow has put in more than all those who are contributing to the offering box. For they all contributed out of their abundance, but she out of her poverty has put in everything she had, all she had to live on."
>
> Mark 12:41–44

The widow had one agenda as she entered the temple: to give *all* that she had. I imagine the keen and watchful eyes of Jesus penetrating the widow's faithful deed and I'm touched by how Jesus saw the intent of her heart. How He lovingly took note of her willingness to come, with no selfish ambitions or plans of withholding of funds. Instead, her hands held fast to her offering—ready to open fully for her master—when it was her turn to give.

It's wonderful to think how Jesus sees our circumstances, the gifts we offer Him, and the full intent of our giving.

I am humbled, in the best way possible, when I think about so many women I've been blessed to meet—women who by the world's standard are classified as the most unlikely to give and the least affluent; but God sees courage when He looks into their lives and their circumstances: divorced, abandoned, single, widowed. They give without regard to their circumstances.

Most of us, if we walked in their shoes, would complain about how awful life is and grumble about a minimum-wage salary or living in a housing development. But like the widow with two coins—a courageous giver—they give beyond their fear for tomorrow's provision. And their joy in giving comes from a deeply rooted trust in God to provide their every need.

The Word of God helps us understand that Jesus wants us to come to Him with generous hearts. He will help us give confidently and freely, from the deepest recesses of our souls, and we will find joy in doing so. This was the difference in the widow woman's giving: It was her absolute joy to bless her Lord. What about you, friend? Our gifts to God are not always monetary. But Jesus sees our heart intent and loves it when we courageously offer Him the best we have. What can you offer to Jesus today that would please His heart? "Good will come to those who are generous" (Psalm 112:5 NIV).

What a generous God we serve. I marvel as He proves himself to be protector, provider, supplier, and so much more for the needs of His people.[2] And I am overcome with gratitude knowing His provisions are perfect in every season of our lives, whether we are old and weak, or strong and youthful. As God rises to take care of us, our souls rise with faithful testimonies overflowing, and we can confidently believe Him for more of the same faithfulness when life looks bleak.

But what about when we are in the middle of our big seasons of blessings and abundance? Do we forget where our help comes from?

My friend Susan courageously confessed to overlooking God in the middle of her greatest financial blessings and abundance. Today her husband is without a job—after several years of unemployment. But my friend faithfully testifies to God's loving care, saying, "I know what it is to live in plenty and I know what it is to live in need. No matter what happens tomorrow, I will never forget God's powerful, daily provision in our greatest times of need."

Courage comes not only to the least affluent, but also to the most affluent who find themselves in unexpected situations but keep their hearts open to an attitude of gratitude. Isn't it wonderful that generosity has nothing to do with how much money we have? A giving life is an abundant life, dear friend.

Sometimes, Generosity Requires Courage

Sometimes I lack the generous spirit of the widow woman and allow my circumstances to cloud my perspective, justifying why I can't give my all. I confess, I am a master of devising some great reasons for not giving, and I sometimes even try to negotiate with God: *Maybe . . . I'll give a little today, Lord; but I promise when money is not so tight I'll give all I can to you.* Sadly, my personal agenda often hinders my ability to be generous because I have plans, dreams, desires—things I want, need, crave. And if I give my all, then what will happen?

How I realize my need for godly women in my life, to lead my heart toward courageous giving. Women like those I mentioned, who live generously in singleness, widowhood, or otherwise, giving freely and lovingly, finding contentment right where they are. And women like Susan, who teach me to be content in every circumstance of life, and the widow woman who trusted God will her all. Oh, how I want to give without expecting anything in return, with no agenda, letting go of fear as I eagerly drop my all into the strong arms of Christ.

> I am not saying this because I am in need, for I have learned to be content whatever the circumstances. I know what it is to be in need, and I know what it is to have plenty. I have learned the secret of being content in any and every situation, whether well fed or hungry, whether living in plenty or in want. I can do all this through him who gives me strength.
>
> Philippians 4:11–13 NIV

What about you, friend? Do you relate? Do you have personal agendas that rob you of your ability to give fully and eagerly to God? When we live tight-fistedly, we run the risk of withholding from God what is rightfully His.

One bright, sunny Sunday morning, my mother gave me some money to put in the offering plate at church. But when she stopped for gas, I hopped out of the car with the money tucked inside my tightly clenched fist, walked into the store, and went up to the candy counter. After selecting my favorite sweet treats, I excitedly hopped back into the car with a small paper bag spilling over with candy, and my pint-sized heart spilling over with joy. The first piece I put into my mouth tasted so delicious, but after a few seconds I could no longer enjoy it. Suddenly, sweet turned bitter and the piece of candy I'd joyfully shoved into my mouth only moments before seemed to get less tasty by the second.

Instead of giving all the money that my mother had designated as God's money, I had used it for my own agenda and selfish desires. This was my first memory of our loving Jesus convicting my heart of wrongdoing. I still think about how I have misused His money at times and I'm convinced of my need for Him to redirect me in how to appropriately use what is His—how to be generous right in the middle of my need.

I was only a child but old enough to understand what it felt like to cheat God, to withhold from Him what was rightfully His. It was a powerful lesson showing me that when we rob God, we rob ourselves too, because selfishness hinders our ability to enjoy the sweet life Jesus came to bless us with.

But even my selfish, childish act didn't change His deep love for me.

I believe that Jesus' love for us runs so wide and deep that on days when we give Him our all, like the widow with the two coins did, or in moments of fear, doubt, and insecurity that convince us to withhold, He loves us still. And He tenderly positions himself, noticing the smallest of generous gestures we make—pleased that we came, courageously *trying*.

On the day the widow came to the temple, Scripture tells us Jesus had positioned himself opposite the temple treasury, in the court of women—the place where individuals gave their offerings. I can't help but wonder what the finely dressed, prestigious women thought of her offering. Did they stare, raise a brow in disgust, or laugh mockingly? Or did they tilt their heads, faces drooping in patronizing pity? Scripture does not give us a window into the widow's soul, but she was a real woman and could have had real emotions warring against her godly best—just like us.

The wealthy women who gathered in the temple court that day might have had all the worldly comforts, but the widow with two coins had unstoppable faith—faith unshaken by the opinions of others. Her faith produced courage to come and give generously. Generosity mattered more than her need to be comfortable. What about you?

Although Scripture gives few details about the widow, we know the courage it takes to trust God when our paycheck is all gone to bills and there are more bills coming in. Without faith, fear might have talked the widow out of giving. Or an entirely different kind of fear might have won. How easy it would have been to shrink back into insecurities, concluding her gift was simply too meager to offer. What if she measured herself against the wealthy women dressed in fine clothing? Have you ever compared yourself with others, coming up short every time? What did the Son of God—Savior of the world who left His mansion in heaven with streets made of pure gold—possibly need with two meager copper coins?

Only the Savior can rescue us from such thoughts. Only Jesus can fill us with enough confidence and courage to believe in the value of our small offerings. I think Jesus is more concerned about our heart condition than the condition of our bank account.

Maybe you measure what you have to give against the extravagant sums others can give, and come up short each time. I so get it! I have experienced the same feelings in my own life but have decided that rather than living closed-handedly, I want to celebrate and give—knowing the same measure of courage granted the widow is available to me. And I have some great news for you: As we faithfully let go, we are choosing to live free—free from self-driven motives whispering, *If I do good things, then God will bless me. If I give more, I will receive more.* Jesus saw what the woman gave and He saw the generosity of her heart, not a restrained heart. And it was measured in full—even more than those who could give so much more.

Are you ready to open your hands, to give out of what you have? If so, I invite you to join me on a personal journey of giving to God all that we are, and all that we have.

At a glance, the amount of money the wealthy dropped into the trumpet-shaped basins might have seemed like an impressive sum, but in truth most likely would have been nothing more than lunch money—at least to them. It doesn't matter whether it is money, talent, or service we are offering; Jesus cares more about the condition of our heart than the amount we offer, or *what* we offer to Him.

Do you think it is possible Jesus identified with the widow in her poverty because He, too, had nothing—not even a stone on which to lay His head? Jesus said to a scribe who approached him: "Foxes have holes, and birds of the air have nests, but the Son of man has nowhere to lay his head" (Matthew 8:20).

Still . . . Jesus gave the best of all He had to offer to us.

What about you? Are you willing to give your best energies to your family first? It's a great way of giving our all to God because we are being good stewards of the people He entrusts to us. Do you have a talent you have been withholding: a beautiful voice, a servant heart, the gift of teaching, speaking, or writing?

Whatever God has given you, give *all* of it back to Him as an act of worship. Like the widow in this story, you might not have much in your hands—but your heart can be so full!

It takes courage for us to step forward, dropping our meager offerings in public places. It takes even more courage to give our *all* when no one is watching: to work hard when the boss is on vacation, to stick with your commitments when no one is there to micro-manage you, to continue your financial giving when you or your spouse has lost a job. As we find courage to overcome our fears and insecurities, our children will learn to be overcomers too.

How do we do this? It might be a monthly plan that you initiate now to automatically designate your tithes or offerings. It could be that you sign up for a weekly or monthly volunteer spot. There are countless ways we can set up an "automatic offering," and I think we will be more intentional with our giving when we do.

God wants to help us become courageous, confident givers who are free in every sense of the word. What we have to offer Him is as unique as our fingerprints, my friend. No one else can offer to God all that *you are*.

Jesus saw the widow's offering as unique and set apart too. Her selfless action was living proof of the courage Christ gives us to live in a "letting go" state of mind. As we let go we are also freeing ourselves to receive the best of all He has for us. The widow woman gave confidently, not as an impoverished woman but a blessed child of God. But sometimes we see our lives as impoverished: Your relationships lack intimacy? Your child has gone astray? Your health is in jeopardy? Your friendships are few? Your finances are in flux? Let's give *all* of these to God as an offering—relinquishing control of the broken and uncertain places of our lives. I think if we aspire to be courageous givers, we must remember that we cannot serve both God and money.[3]

I wish we could sit with the widow with two coins and hear the rest of her life story—how after abandoning her worries over tomorrow's bread, Jesus, heaven's authority, proved faithful. He was her retirement plan and He will take care of our futures too. Her Jesus-shaped heart surrendered to His authority—all because of love. And her generosity set heaven in motion with good measure pressed down, shaken together, running over with blessings.[4] Little did the Pharisees know that when she walked through the temple doors, courage came too.

As a five-year-old girl, I sat each week anxiously waiting for COURAGE to walk through the door leading to the Sunday school class. Mrs. Fountain was one of the most loving and selfless women I had ever known. As a widow, she faithfully served her family, her community, and our small country church—making her five-year-old Sunday school class a main priority. Her generous heart was evidenced by a willingness to spend her last dime, if necessary, supplying us hungry little munchkins with plenty of Cheetos and Kool-Aid.

Sunday mornings were filled with wonder and excitement, and I was most concerned with arriving as early as possible to claim my favorite red chair. Despite the many years that have passed, I still smile when recounting kind offerings Mrs. Fountain made as she invested her time and energy, giving us the best of all she had each week. God's love proved big in my little five-year-old heart because of one widow's faithfulness. I am living proof that Mrs. Fountain's sacrifices paid off, and I often wish she were alive so I could tell her so.

I loved and appreciated her back then, but it wasn't until I became a woman that I truly understood the gravity of her meager circumstances and how she generously gave beyond them. But I know Jesus took note of it all, just like He took note of the widow with two coins. And just like He takes note of your daily sacrifices: the meals prepared for your family, the cake you bake for the depressed woman down the street, the handwritten note you thoughtfully penned to a struggling teenager, the loving hug you gave to a child, the clothes you donated to the family who lost everything when their home burned down. All of this God takes note of because He knows how crazy busy and jam-packed our lives are. He knows how poverty-stricken our souls become when we are stressed and undone by uncontrollable circumstances in life, and He sees our offerings glistening in the light of His love, much like the widow with two coins.

Tears fill my eyes as I reminisce about how deeply Mrs. Fountain's godly influence managed to stamp its way into my heart. More than ever, I respect the courage it must have taken to trust in God's provision while selflessly indulging a group of sometimes poorly behaved five-year-old hungry piglets with treats while on a fixed income. And thinking about how she even got to church was another factor. There must have been times of fear. Things must have seemed scary. If so, she never seemed afraid. In fact, the twinkle in her eyes when she taught us about Jesus revealed the source of her faith-filled confidence and her reason for joyfully giving. Each week, as she opened her hands, giving to God all she had—she opened my little heart—making me want to give Him all that I had too!

I loved her dramatic recounts and how her eyes lit up with excitement as she told stories about the courage of Mary, Martha, Deborah, and David. Daniel in the lion's den kept me on the edge of my seat, and John the Baptist paved the way for Jesus to come into my heart. Although I didn't understand it then, I surely understand now: Mrs. Fountain was courage personified. It didn't matter that she had little more than an elementary school education. Jesus supplied all the wisdom and knowledge needed. She brought her gift and gave it joyfully—all of it, without holding anything back. When others refused—wanting more visible, back-slapping, praise-filled positions in the church—Mrs. Fountain kept giving all she had to her Lord, much like the widow with two coins. I think she would have spent her last dime and gone without a few meals to make sure we had our beloved snacks each week.

Giving What You Have, As You Are, Takes Courage

Remember: It doesn't matter what we look like when we come to Him with our offerings. Courage came to me, week after week, in a calico-printed dress and Hush Puppies shoes—her hair twisted neatly in a bun on top of her head. Courage can be lived out in my life and in yours as we generously give God our all in faded jeans and tattered T-shirts, in tennis shoes or flip-flops, with hair tangled or combed neatly. With much to give or little to offer. An ounce of time or a bit more. It isn't the size of the gift, but the position of our hearts when we give.

I hope knowing this will remind you to courageously give all that you are, just as you are. Your heart may be filled with doubts and questions: *How can I give to God when my children want to go to college? What can I give when my husband left me with five children to raise alone and no income? What do I do when intimidation wars against generosity?*

The answer, my friend, is to give as the Lord impresses, as much or as little as He impresses.

Give generously, friend. To give begrudgingly is to give in vain. But as we come to God as joyful givers, like the widow with two coins, then our giving becomes a beautiful act of worship. Doesn't God deserve our best attitudes, our best energies, and the first fruits of our time? Let's be creative in our giving to Him.

Perhaps we can

- Volunteer at a nursing home
- Help a friend in need
- Give to the man holding the sign by the roadside—trusting God with the outcome

- Pay for the person's food one car behind in the fast-food drive-through line
- Tip the waitress double what you normally would
- Donate clothing and other home items to those in need
- Hold the hand of someone who is grieving

God has a provision plan for your life that is unmatched, unchangeable, and unshakable. Will you commit to giving in the most unlikely of places, in the most unlikely of ways? As we drop our offerings, may they shimmer in the watchful eyes of the Savior's light—knowing our little becomes great when we give our all for God.

I'm convinced God is looking for a few good, courageous women to love selflessly, to give without second-guessing, and to bless and serve the world we live in.

COURAGE QUEST

1. Read Mark 12:41–44 and imagine yourself in the temple court bringing the best you have to offer Jesus. What's in your hand, friend?
2. What have you been clinging tightly to? Time, money, comforts, friends, control, talents, your children? List treasures in your hand that you struggle to release to God's best keeping.
3. How is releasing the things we hold on to a most powerful act of worship?
4. Do you lack courage to trust that your needs will be provided for tomorrow, if you give today?
5. How does the widow's courage inspire you to give beyond what you think possible?

4

What's in Your Hand?

As the heavy rain pelted Jael's tent, its rhythmic pitter-patter must have paled in comparison to the questions battering her mind. The rains were flooding the Kishon Valley near where she and her Kenite husband, Heber, had pitched their tent.[1] But where was he? Wouldn't any woman wonder and be on edge, having heard the distant sounds of Canaan's army marching to the valley of Tabor in hot pursuit of the Israelite nation?

If you remember from chapter 1, "Man Up and Lead!," Barak had asked courageous Judge Deborah to go into battle with him because he was afraid—intimidated by an enemy named Sisera and his nine hundred iron chariots. Deborah agreed to go with him, but told Barak the enemy would be given over into the hands of a woman.[2] Surely Deborah had spoken of herself?

But Jael might have wondered how a woman could accomplish such a thing. In a culture where women were considered second-class, this must have been unimaginable. Still, Deborah's capabilities were obvious to Jael. She was brave, strong, and wise. (It's easy for us to see the strong points in others, while overlooking our own, isn't it?) Thinking about Deborah's courageous spirit must have encouraged Jael and made her proud to be a woman.

Meanwhile, in divinely appointed timing, Barak's attack of Sisera's forces coincided with the heavy rains, when the river was swollen, overflowing its banks and turning the ground into sticky mud. We are told in the Song of Deborah, "'The river of Kishon swept them away, that ancient river, the river Kishon'" (Judges 5:21 NIV). What a perfect plan God devised! Sisera's heavy armored chariots would be neutralized—sinking into the mud, right before Barak's eyes.

> And Deborah said to Barak, "Up! For this is the day in which the Lord has given Sisera into your hand. Does not the Lord go out before you?" So Barak went down from Mount Tabor with 10,000 men following him. And the Lord routed Sisera and all his chariots and all his army before Barak by the edge of the sword. And Sisera got down from his chariot and fled away on foot. And Barak pursued the chariots and the army to Harosheth-hagoyim, and all the army of Sisera fell by the edge of the sword; not a man was left.
>
> Judges 4:14–16

While Deborah and Barak's main concern was fighting the battle, Heber, Jael's husband, likely sought to remain neutral, as we'll see shortly. *His* main concern probably was with keeping peace with both the Canaanite and the Israelite nations. We don't know if Heber's peacemaking ways were fear-driven, or were his way of wisely ensuring their safety. Nomadic living demanded repetitive upheaval—relocating of their tents, their animals, and every possession they owned.

As the battle sounds intensified, I can almost see Jael's work-worn hands feverishly tightening the laces of the tent opening. Setting up camp was considered woman's work, and her fingers were strong, agile, and so familiar with this labor-intensive routine she could have done it with her eyes closed. I imagine Jael pushing piles of clay dishes this way and that—nervously busying herself to push worry aside. Did she wonder if her husband's peacemaking ways would bring the battle to their front door?

And as Jael reflected on the division of her nation, do you think it dawned on her how it might mirror division in her own household? Jael must have had a good grip on how dangerous tent-dwelling life could be and would have understood the importance of pitching their tent in friendly territories.

As she slowly turned back to warm her weary bones by the fire, her thoughts were interrupted by the sound of footsteps outside her tent. They were quick and intentional. But were they friendly, or not? Jael would soon find out:

> Sisera, meanwhile, fled on foot to the tent of Jael, the wife of Heber the Kenite, because there was an alliance between Jabin king of Hazor and the family of Heber the Kenite.
>
> Judges 4:17

Jael must have centered herself, focusing on the moment. Do you think she whispered under her breath, "Heber, where are you when I need you most? Look where your schmoozing with the enemy has gotten us! Of course, the enemy would assume he'd be welcome here!"

So what's a girl to do when a surprise visitor shows up? Invite him in, of course. What happens next is a surprising twist of events in a story that began with courageous Deborah and ends with courageous Jael:

> And Jael came out to meet Sisera and said to him, "Turn aside, my lord; turn aside to me; do not be afraid." So he turned aside to her into the tent, and she covered him with a rug. And he said to her, "Please give me a little water to drink, for I am thirsty." So she opened a skin of milk and gave him a drink and covered him. And he said to her, "Stand at the opening of the tent, and if any man comes and asks you, 'Is anyone here?' say, 'No.'" But Jael the wife of Heber took a tent peg, and took a hammer in her hand. Then she went softly to him and drove the peg into his temple until it went down into the ground while he was lying fast asleep from weariness. So he died. And behold, as Barak was pursuing Sisera, Jael went out to meet him and said to him, "Come, and I will show you the man whom you are seeking." So he went in to her tent, and there lay Sisera dead, with the tent peg in his temple.
>
> Judges 4:17–22

If you remember from chapter 1, Deborah goes courageously into battle after telling Barak that the enemy would be delivered into the hands of a woman. Now we see that woman is not Deborah but Jael.

How could Jael have known when she woke that morning that God was about to use her strong, capable, tent-pitching hands to defeat one of Israel's most dangerous enemies—Sisera, the Canaanite, commander of King Jabin's army? I doubt many of us know how God wants to use *us* and all He can do through us, if we will look for opportunities to be included in His plan.

When the Fearful Become the Courageously Free

I like to think about the women in my family lineage whom I never had the privilege of meeting, wondering how God used them, and it is fun to imagine the lives of women in the Bible also! Let's grow together as we imagine what Jael looked like, how she might have felt about her nomadic lifestyle, and how much courage it must have taken for her to overcome her fears and insecurities for a life of confidence and freedom.

It was a woman named Deborah who spoke on that fateful day when Barak shrank back in fear. It was Deborah who courageously stepped up when Barak failed to man up and lead. And everything happened exactly as God planned.

It was a woman named Jael who slew the enemy—right inside her home. And it's women like you and me who can learn from women like Deborah and Jael and be the next in line for God to use miraculously.

Friend, God opportunities require faithful action from willing people. Our occasional lack of courage promotes fear and complacency. But our supremely capable God enables us to overcome when daunting circumstances are drowning our courage.

Jael proved herself bold, willing, and capable on that prophetic day when God caused it to rain so hard that the Kishon River flooded, leaving the Canaanite army panicked and undone. Sisera abandoned his army and his nine hundred horse-drawn chariots to save himself—running to his ally Heber's tent, his power and his pride literally stuck in the mud.

Of all things, rain! Really? Yep, rain! This wasn't God's first rodeo. He'd used rainwaters in the book of Genesis, providing Noah and his family and all the animals a way of escape.[3] They would not sink, but float. Because one man, Noah, had listened carefully to God's instructions and acted courageously by faith, when others laughed in his face. The same God who protected Noah, Deborah, and Jael also protects you and me, friend.

Imagine God at work in your life. Now, breathe in rest for your weary soul. Because it's true! He is at work, even when your circumstances seem to be drowning you, or when you feel stuck—not in the Kishon River, but in the muddy waters of a river of regret. Look for God. You will surely find Him. And as you courageously put your trust in Him, Satan will tuck his tail between his fearful legs and run for his life in an undone panic—like Sisera did.

But sometimes the enemy runs right to our door. And like the Israelite nation's, our battles often begin years before our victories and are based on how we live our lives. It takes courage to believe help is on the way, when the battle sounds are loud, costly, and demanding. It takes courage to come out of our hiding place, like Jael, to courageously face our circumstances.

What was Jael to do when Sisera showed up? Hospitality was a highly honored tradition among desert tent dwellers. But what a risk she took, inviting the commanding officer of King Jabin's powerful army into her tent. When I think about the meaning of Jael's name, "wild or mountain goat," I can understand how her actions, as wild as they may have seemed, were used as part of God's big plan. This shows that our God will use even our "crazy" if we are willing to be used by Him.

Centuries before the fateful day when Jael picked up the tent stake and drove it into the head of Israel's enemy for the nation's protection and freedom, God had challenged Moses to use what was in his hand to perform miracles that would set the stage for God's chosen people to be freed from four hundred years of bondage and persecution. God asked Moses:

> "What is that in your hand?" He said, "A staff."
>
> Exodus 4:1–2

And who would have ever imagined that a simple wooden staff and an ounce of courageous faith could part the waters of the Red Sea and usher a nation to freedom?[4]

I wonder how our own lives might bring power and freedom to the world in which we live. Let's think about what God has placed in our hands and how we might use it to encourage, bless, and free others from daily stress and discouragement. Our "staff" might be a talent we've hidden behind our back, but God is saying, "What's in your hand, friend?"

You might be thinking, *LaTan, you have no idea how little talent I have.* Well, friend, can you knit? Then pick up your knitting needles and make something for someone who is sick. Can you cook? Then pick up that spatula and bake something for a friend who has lost a loved one. Can you write? Pick up your pretty pen and write a note of encouragement to someone struggling with depression. Can you clean? Pick up that toilet brush and clean the bathroom for someone who has gone through surgery or chemo. If you can sing, pick up the phone and sing a song of praise over a soul who has lost hope of believing God loves them. Can you smile? Then remind your face to do so and make someone's day by flashing your pearly whites their way.

What's that in your hand, my friend? Use it courageously! Every ounce of it—to the glory of God. Let your Jael-wild, mountain-goat, spirit-girl "go" courageously toward God's best leading. Let the Almighty decide if it's treacherously crazy—or a blessing and a gloriously courageous act of obedience with the potential to free others for the next twenty years, as Jael's courageous actions did. The world needs your flavor of crazy. There's no one like you!

You are so precious to God. He knows every fiber of your being and treasures each one. No matter what your life looks like today, no matter what issues you are dealing with, no matter how far gone you think your circumstances are, God still has His pen in His holy hand and I think He wants us to courageously participate in a great story that He is writing across the pages of our lives. The enemy cannot stand against a woman who is willing to courageously act in obedience. But God wants us to be consistent in faith, not tossed about emotionally when the battles seem overwhelming or the enemy is on our front porch step.

Sometimes I get sick of my inability to remain consistently courageous. I've asked the Lord, many times, "Lord, if I am this sick and tired of me, how can you not be?" But His love endures forever, and I am so grateful, aren't you?[5] I find rest in knowing I am *becoming* something more . . . day by day, as God faithfully writes my story and transforms my life into His divine plan and purpose.

Both Deborah and Jael had been given leading roles in God's divine plan and purpose to save and rescue the nation He so loved. The nation God has given me and you is found in our families who gather around our tables. The little arms that lovingly wrap themselves around us, the tiny noses pressed hard against our necks. Those visiting for holidays, whose crazy got the best of them and they've gone astray.

Jael not only defended her nation, she defended her divided household. What about you? Are you building a home that will last—knowing which side you are fighting for, making wise decisions that will bring blessings to your entire household? It takes courage to do this, but you can do it!

Has there ever been a time in your life when you and your spouse were divided in some way? Religious beliefs, political views, parenting standards? We know from Scripture that Jael's house/tent was divided politically. If she and Heber were going to the polls to vote, Jael's vote would have cancelled out Heber's for sure. Do you argue incessantly with your husband about every silly little thing—just for the sake of being right? It takes courage to start fresh, pitch a new tent, and secure the stakes of your home by trusting God with your past, present, and future wars. But it will be so worth it! A united marriage results in a united home front, friend.

But perhaps you've been forced to make decisions for your tent/home and have grown weary of bearing the entire financial or spiritual weight on your shoulders. You just want a man to lead you. Instead of being a helpmate you've been forced to lead. Take courage: God will be your leading man. If you are single, pursue the heart of God; the rainwaters of God's spirit will fill you, and you'll spend less time disappointed in a man because God is on your side, leading and fighting for you. If you are married to a complacent or faithless man who lacks courage, commit yourself to praying for him daily. As you do this, God will strengthen and help you wait for your man to rise to his best, his God-given appointment as head of your home, and God will be your husband in the waiting.

Courage for Daily Living

If we want to live and act courageously, it's so important for us to keep a close relationship with God. He will help us exemplify courageous living. He offers compassion when we feel fearful of what's ahead. Will you align your heart with His today, friend? We must carefully and prayerfully align our lives with the spirit of God and then with strong people of faith who lean hard into His power and are fearless because of the power at work in their lives. By pitching our tents near these people, we will become better, stronger, wiser people.

> Now Heber the Kenite had separated from the Kenites, the descendants of Hobab the father-in-law of Moses, and had pitched his tent as far away as the oak in Zaanannim, which is near Kedesh.
>
> Judges 4:11

Scripture doesn't tell us why Heber chose to move—separating himself from his family/tribe. The only thing we know is there was trouble in what was supposed to be paradise—Canaan—the place God had wanted to bring absolute peace to His people. Do you bring your troubled life to God and include Him in every decision of your life? If not, let's start today! When we do, such decisions won't create turmoil or invite the enemy to our door, as the poor decisions of the Israelite nation invited the enemy in. But when the enemy does come knocking, he will find our home, our lives, and our circumstances covered in the power of prayer. Instead of making him comfortable, covering him with a furry afghan after giving him hot cocoa, and singing our whiney lullabies, our courageous lives will make him miserable, because he will see that our great God is our battle instructor.

When money is tight and patience is growing thin, when the enemy's voice is loud and your head hurts from the chaos and noise of your own thoughts, when you feel alone or afraid and ill equipped, pick up the Word of God, ready yourself with this most powerful stake in your hand. Fight courageously for a sweet, positive attitude and selfless actions. It takes courage to believe that tomorrow will be better.

Don't allow yourself to give in to the enemy's blame game. I wonder if Jael blamed Heber for making her move so many times? Have you ever blamed your husband for taking the job in some distant land/city—far from the people you know and love? Away from the church family you felt oneness with? The fantastic friends you could totally be yourself with, who you could literally look at and know what they were thinking?

After pitching your tent (setting up house), the glitter falls away and loneliness sets in. You unpack The Blame Game, dust it off, and begin faulting your husband for taking you to some God-forsaken land. You love this game. It feels empowering to remind him of the beautiful life you left behind. We must be so careful not to allow our misery to become someone else's punishment.

Years ago, just before giving birth to our third child, our family moved across town to a larger tent (home). I was nine months pregnant with little time to drive the stakes in deep (ready our house) for the arrival of our newest family member. I felt fat and grew more exhausted with each box I unpacked, taking lots of breaks in the pantry, consoling myself with the fact that we had *no intention of ever moving again*. Feeling extra satisfied, I hammered my emotional stakes down firmly, feeling a bit like nomadic Jael. This was our eighth move in eleven years of marriage. I was especially grateful for my tribe (mother and sister), who had traveled from their distant land (Georgia) to help me tighten the straps of our tent, so to speak. I was ever so grateful for their willingness to use the gifts of their hands to lovingly unpack the many boxes. No more nomadic dwellings. We were home, at last.

NOT!

After four months in our new dream home, my husband received a call: an irresistible job offer in the foreign land of Raleigh, North Carolina, where we knew *no one*. I forced myself to focus on all the perks of moving: more money, bigger and brand-new house, in a golf-course community with a pool, etc. . . . We packed up the camel (white Honda Accord) with everything that wouldn't fit inside the U-Haul truck and left for our new life adventure.

But our dreams were dashed before we even made the turn onto our new street. Yellow plastic tape stretched across the pond behind the house reading: POLICE LINE: DO NOT CROSS! Suddenly, our blessed promised land felt like a land of curses, especially when we heard the news that an unidentified body had been found floating in the lake behind our newly raised tent (custom-built home).

Much as the Israelite nation experienced, what we thought would be the land of peace seemed scary and uncertain. I wish I could tell you that I courageously drove the stakes in the ground, using strong faith-filled hands. Oh, how my pride would love to convince you that when my husband left to go to work each day—working late into the nights—I courageously supported him and drove the stakes deeper in prayer. But the truth is, fear gripped my heart with concern for our personal safety, and I was consumed with loneliness, wanting to go home, back to the familiar faces we so loved.

I felt the most alone I'd ever felt, in this new land of anonymity. With three children to care for while my husband went to work for extended hours, I had no one to talk to. A war started raging in my mind, and courage was nowhere to be found. Like I stated before, sometimes we create our own wars. In my case, the battlefield looked like a poorly dressed housewife who got lost in her personal pain, letting herself go by eating a poor diet to fill the empty void.

But I am so grateful that the same God who helped Deborah and Jael was there to help me. I found that the best way to conquer this new land and the enemy who ran for my door was to be others-minded. My children and I picked up the stake—I mean the cookie spatula—and baked dozens of cookies to deliver to the other tribes moving into our newly developed neighborhood. Using what was in our hands we combatted loneliness and comforted many others who were also struggling with their move to a new city. Soon, our hearts and our home were full of new friends, laughter, and love.

Your enemy comes to rob and destroy and kill, but Jesus came that we might have life, and have it to the full.[6] Don't let Satan fill your mind with dark regrets of how much better yesterday was and how tomorrow will never be the same. Keep in mind there's a red line just across the lake behind your tent/house that reads, GOD'S TERRITORY: DO NOT CROSS. And the dead body will be Satan's when God gives one woman, *you,* the final victory.

Christ made a way for you and your tribe/family—the little nation He has entrusted you to lead into peaceful living. He wants you to have all the blessings of heaven—the whole kit and caboodle. He wants you to walk in true freedom and experience the promised land, right where you are, as you are. Never forget that one willing woman with a tiny ounce of faith, grit, and tenacity can do amazing things; there is nothing too big, too hard, or too impossible with God.[7]

I can't wrap this chapter up without asking: Have you chosen Jesus Christ as your Savior? If not, it's never too late! It's so simple. It starts with a willing heart and a prayer that goes something like this:

> *Father, I don't understand all that you are, but the power of your holy Word has my attention and I want to live a courageous life of faith in you. I thank you for the gift of your Son, Jesus, whose death and resurrection have reconciled me to you. Forgive me of my sin, and come into my heart, Lord. Take up every empty space. I offer every part of who I am to you. Take my heart and life captive as your territory. Amen.*

God's Word is the tool in your hand to conquer those complacent, neutral mindsets. Remember, a divided heart often creates a divided home. By not choosing Christ, we've already chosen who we will serve. Choose Christ; He will show us great and marvelous things—things we could never realize without His power.[8] He is available to speak to our deepest, most intimate places of need. Let's fix our hearts on courageous living, friend, taking notes from Jael. We have so much to learn from her about how to allow God to use us right where we are. The mundane, repetitive, dreaded tasks we are responsible for inside the walls of our tent/home can be big blessings for others. Don't underestimate God's ability to make your life powerful. Let go of today's fear and walk confidently into tomorrow's courage.

So, what's in *your* hand, friend?

COURAGE QUEST

1. Read Judges 5 and think about the enemy being handed over to a woman. What a powerful reminder to us, as women, that we are not helpless in our struggles with circumstances and people.
2. How does Jael inspire you to be more intentional about protecting your home from the enemy, Satan?
3. What can you do to protect yourself from the enemy who wants to destroy your marriage, your children, your home?
4. What has God placed in your hand that could bring blessings and protection to your family?
5. Are you willing to allow God to use you in the mundane repetition of living?

5

Own Your Tomorrows

I wonder if Abigail turned her back to the servant nervously clamoring on about how poorly her husband, Nabal, had treated David's troops while camped in the Wilderness of Paran? Scripture doesn't tell us whether the messenger ran to tell Abigail or went slowly, but we hear his disgust in his report:

> "David sent messengers from the wilderness to give our master his greetings, but he hurled insults at them. Yet these men were very good to us. They did not mistreat us, and the whole time we were out in the fields near them nothing was missing. Night and day they were a wall around us all the time we were herding our sheep near them. Now think it over and see what you can do, because disaster is hanging over our master and his whole household. He is such a wicked man that no one can talk to him."
>
> 1 Samuel 25:14–17 NIV

Imagine Abigail graciously thanking the young messenger, waving good-bye with a halfhearted smile. Did she bite her lip to hold back the seething anger consuming her as she replayed each embarrassing piece of his detailed report? Did disbelief wash over her as she realized Nabal had done it . . . again? Her husband's usual wicked demeanor must have been more than Abigail could stand. I think it was *usual* because how else can we explain a servant grumbling *about* his master *to his master's wife*? If familiarity breeds contempt, then Nabal's bad behavior must not have come as a surprise. Nabal was known for belittling others with his quick, harsh, and cutting gestures:

> "Who is this David? Who is this son of Jesse?"
>
> 1 Samuel 25:10 NIV

Abigail's husband had sarcastically smirked in response to David's request for food and provisions. Can you envision Nabal sizing up the ten young men David had sent—from head to toe? Nabal's condescending response was unjustifiable! The men had greeted Nabal respectfully, their demeanor as kind as David's message itself:

> "Long life to you! Good health to you and your household! And good health to all that is yours! Now I hear that it is sheep-shearing time. When your shepherds were with us, we did not mistreat them, and the whole time they were at Carmel nothing of theirs was missing. Ask your own servants and they will tell you. Therefore be favorable toward my young men, since we come at a festive time. Please give your servants and your son David whatever you can find for them."
>
> 1 Samuel 25:5–8 NIV

Abigail didn't need to ask Nabal's servants; they had willingly brought the news of Nabal's arrogance to her—proof that Abigail had won the respect of Nabal's entire household. What woman living in Abigail's day could possibly change an overbearing, unwise man's decision? Evidently, the tattling servant thought Abigail could. Friend, godly character can't be tucked away; it's on display—for the world to see—whether we are outspoken or shy. I think Abigail's integrity spoke for itself.

I realize your goal in life might not be to become a leader; I'm not sure it was Abigail's either. But when others see character, integrity, and courage in you, they automatically see a leader too! Abigail's story should give us the desire to become the best version of ourselves we can possibly be, knowing others are depending on us to have big courage when life gets hard. Some of us have been assigned to cantankerous parents, mothers-in-law, sisters-in-law, children, friends, co-workers, and bosses. I truly feel for Abigail, assigned to cantankerous Nabal. It takes courage to keep it together when others have created upheaval all around us.

Sometimes it's hard to do the right thing when stronger, overbearing personalities try to control or dominate our situations. But we don't have to allow these difficult people to destroy our tomorrows. Remember, Satan roams around like a roaring lion seeking to devour us and he can spot fear and frustration in us a mile away. He works hard to fill our lives with anxiety, using people in our own families to cause the most upheaval of all. His goal is to destroy any possible opportunity for peaceful living.

> Keep a cool head. Stay alert. The Devil is poised to pounce, and would like nothing better than to catch you napping. Keep your guard up. You're not the only ones plunged into these hard times. It's the same with Christians all over the world. So keep a firm grip on the faith. The suffering won't last forever. It won't be long before this generous God who has great plans

> for us in Christ—eternal and glorious plans they are!—will have you put together and on your feet for good. He gets the last word; yes, he does.
>
> 1 Peter 5:8 MESSAGE

Courageous Attitudes Bring Courageous Actions

Abigail's selfish husband had caused upheaval all right! And David was on his way to destroy Nabal's entire household.[1] But I love how Abigail chose to have an attitude of courage before ever acting courageously. Everything she did was with careful planning. Abigail had a firm grip on her faith, and God put her frayed nerves back together and put her on her feet, and she busily prepared for her journey:

> Abigail acted quickly. She took two hundred loaves of bread, two skins of wine, five dressed sheep, five seahs of roasted grain, a hundred cakes of raisins and two hundred cakes of pressed figs, and loaded them on donkeys. Then she told her servants, "Go on ahead; I'll follow you." But she did not tell her husband Nabal.
>
> 1 Samuel 25:18–19 NIV

As she journeyed along, do you think she replayed Nabal's rudeness? I do—knowing how we women sometimes have trouble letting things go. Questions might have filled Abigail with more disgust: *How dare Nabal respond so rudely to David's request for food? I can't believe he said,*

> "Shall I take my bread, my water, and my meat that I have killed for my shearers and give it to men who come from I do not know where?"
>
> 1 Samuel 25:11

How dare he pretend not to know who David, son of Jesse, is! David's success had won him a high ranking in the army of King Saul.[2]

There was no time for blame. Nabal's lack of respect and carelessness had put their lives in danger, and positioned Abigail on the back of a donkey in hopes of making yesterday's wrongs right.

> As she came riding her donkey into a mountain ravine, there were David and his men descending toward her, and she met them. David had just said, "It's been useless—all my watching over this fellow's property in the desert so that nothing of his was missing. He has paid me back evil for good. May God deal with David, be it ever so severely, if by morning I leave alive one male of all who belong to him!"
>
> 1 Samuel 25:20–21 NIV

Friend, if it's hard for you to imagine how Nabal's actions could have caused such a ruckus, then perhaps you've never experienced the company of a brash, angry person. Lucky you! Scripture paints a very vivid picture, offering full details of just how brash Abigail's husband was. Abigail knew it, the servant knew it—and he was "over it"—telling Abigail, "He is such a wicked man that no one can talk to him" (1 Samuel 15:17 NIV).

Nabal had pushed David's buttons, resulting in David's hot pursuit of him. But Abigail went courageously to meet David, knowing her life and the lives of others depended on her.

Perhaps it was the memory of David's gracious message sent to Nabal that had somehow eased Abigail's fears, giving her courage in going before such a high-ranking military leader. After all, he had told the ten messengers to

> "Go up to Carmel, and go to Nabal and greet him in my name. And thus, you shall greet him: 'Peace be to you, and peace be to your house, and peace be to all that you have.'"
>
> 1 Samuel 25:5–6

Surely Nabal had common sense enough to know that his response had been out of line and was offensive in every way. David's tenderness, on the other hand, would move any girl's heart to action, right? We might wonder how Abigail, a woman with both brains and beauty, could end up with a guy like Nabal.[3] The contrast between her beauty and Nabal's ugly spirit is sharp, mirroring our ugly spirits in contrast to our sweet Jesus. Beautiful Abigail represented ugly Nabal's case before David, to remove the sting of impending death coming for her people, and Jesus did the same when He *became* the curse for us, giving His life for ours on the cross.[4]

Wouldn't you want to repay David and his troops for keeping watch over your household—over the people you care about, putting a wall around your most valuable possession? This is what David did for Nabal and his shepherds while away, and this is what the Lord does for us, dear one. He hems us in.[5] He covers us with His feathers.[6] Protects us and our families—day and night. My heart is full, thinking of these blessings, and it makes me want to bring my best to God, to lavish Him with everything I can possibly scrape together. Because sometimes my life feels like scraps. What about you?

Abigail used the wealth endowed to her, bringing the best provisions from yesterday's storehouse, along with her beautiful humility, to the mountain ravine. And her timing was impeccable, because David had just finished grumbling about how Nabal had repaid his good with evil, expressing his oath to annihilate everyone who belonged to him.[7] By this point I'm guessing Abigail's face was dust-covered from her travels, yet beautiful nonetheless. Friend, when the predicaments others cause place us on a dusty, dirty, fearful path, keep this in mind: Nothing can taint our godly beauty. Because God sees our heart, when man sees our outward appearance.[8]

Approaching David, Abigail quickly dismounted her donkey, then bowed before him with her face to the ground:

> "Pardon your servant, my lord, and let me speak to you; hear what your servant has to say. Please pay no attention, my lord, to that wicked man Nabal. He is just like his name—his name means Fool and folly goes with him. And as for me, your servant, I did not see the men my lord sent."
>
> 1 Samuel 25:24–25 NIV

Can you see Abigail in your mind? Can you hear the humility of her heart speaking to David?

> "The good person out of the good treasure of his heart produces good, and the evil person out of his evil treasure produces evil, for out of the abundance of the heart his mouth speaks."
>
> Luke 6:45

Placing blame, making excuses, or trying to manipulate her situation wouldn't have worked well in convincing David to retreat. Instead, Abigail courageously spoke truth to the one who could save her life, her redeemer, David. I love that she didn't tell a lie, water down the truth, or make excuses for Nabal's arrogance. Instead, she referred to him by the character in which he lived: *a fool*. In ancient Israel names were often connected to a person's character. Whether Nabal was given this name or earned it, he did live up to it.[9] But Abigail was no fool! She knew generosity demanded courage, much like the widow woman in the previous chapter.

Did sweat fall from Abigail's brow as she humbly bowed before David? Did she hold her breath, pray not to be beheaded? We don't know. But, we do know her actions were honorable and courageous, and David's response tells us that he was moved by Abigail's humility and bravery:

> And David said to Abigail. "Blessed be the lord, the God of Israel, who sent you this day to meet me! Blessed be your discretion, and blessed be you who have kept me this day from bloodguilt and from working salvation with my own hand! For as surely as the Lord, the God of Israel, lives, who has restrained me from hurting you, unless you had hurried and come to meet me, truly by morning there had not been left to Nabal so much as one male." Then David received from her hand what she had brought him. And he said to her, "Go up in peace to your house. See, I have obeyed your voice, and I have granted your petition."
>
> 1 Samuel 25:32–35

Most of us would have been tempted to run back to our husband with an in-his-face *Na, na, na, na, na!* But I think Abigail knew, without a doubt, that if it hadn't been for God's supernatural help, she would not have been able to courageously take another painstaking, fearful step toward her hope—her redeemed tomorrow. What about you? How would your victory have caused you to respond?

Abigail waited, once again, for God's perfect timing, before telling Nabal what she'd done. Partly because he was drunk when she returned from her mercy journey.[10] After hearing the news, Nabal's "heart failed him and he became like a stone. About ten days later, the Lord struck Nabal and he died" (1 Samuel 25:37–38 NIV).

One of my all-time favorite verses in the Bible says:

> And to make it your ambition to live a quiet life. You should mind your own business and work hard with your hands, just as we told you, so that your daily life may win the respect of outsiders and so that you will not be dependent on anyone.
>
> 1 Thessalonians 4:11–12 NIV

Abigail's beautiful, quiet restraint helped her to take courage even when she could not depend on her husband to make yesterday's wrongs right. With godly humility, she resourcefully worked toward creating better tomorrows for herself, her family, and friends, and in doing so won the respect of soldiers, servants, and soon-to-be-king David. Her painful journey would have required a special kind of faith to walk out.

It Takes Courage to Walk by Faith

On a recent trip, I excitedly slipped on my new wedge-heeled shoes. They. Were. Adorable. And I was pleased they felt so comfortable since I'd have long walks between airport gates. But after walking awhile, excruciating pain set in. With blistered toes I struggled along, the pain so intense I could barely breathe. A random thought occurred to me: I would practice Lamaze breathing techniques—the ones I'd learned but never used during childbirth but that had come in handy when my children were learning to drive.

I proceeded to breathe in and out, in rhythmic tones to keep my mind off the pain: *Hee, hee, hoo,* until . . . I found a *trash can.* Yep, I threw my cute shoes away in a flash, and was happy I'd brought along my comfortable, ugly flats. I was confused by how my shoes could have created such painful blisters, and in such a short time. They were so comfy while I was standing still.

I think there's a powerful truth here for us today, and one that Abigail would understand: It's the "walk" that's the true test and often the most painful in our faith journey. What about you? Do you throw your spiritual shoes in the trash when life gets hard? Abigail didn't. Her life was challenging, but I think she had a decided heart—wanting more for her life than yesterday's troubles. Courage helped her to conquer her fears and insecurities. My friend, whether you are rich or poor or somewhere in between, don't allow a selfish spirit to block the path leading to your future freedoms.

No matter our income level, we do have riches, or resources, to share, as this commentary sums up:

> There are four kinds of riches. There are riches in what you *have,* riches in what you *do*, riches in what you *know*, and riches in what you *are*—riches in *character*. Nabal was a very rich man, but only rich in what he had.[11]

Nabal owned one thousand goats and three thousand sheep[12]—his life blessed with abundance. There was no excuse for such rudeness or his selfish spirit. Is there any excuse for our selfishness?

You won't believe this! I literally just received a text message from a friend asking if she could borrow some of my home decor to help a missionary living in our area to cut wedding costs. I responded with: *"I am so sorry, I have an event going on that same weekend at my house, and I don't want to dismantle my house before my guest arrives."* My response was so unlike me. Although I did want our home to look nice when my guest arrived, I failed to notice the *my, my, my:* "*My* friends are coming, I will need *my* decorating items for *my* house." I thought about how this opportunity given to me was like David's ten men asking Nabal for provisions when they were in dire need.

Although I am not a rich woman, I am blessed with many items I've used to decorate for weddings in times past. My usually generous spirit had been overshadowed by a me-minded attitude. I called my friend immediately, telling her I'd gladly load my donkey (Toyota Highlander) with provisions to supply this very real need. And I pray that God will help each of us live generously, whether emptying our cupboards for a single mother in need or stripping the decor from the walls of our home for a missionary bride-to-be. I might have failed my Nabal test, but I will work hard to pass my Abigail test, on every tomorrow. Will you bless others with what you have? Are you willing to deliver your blessings to others, knowing you are blessed to be a blessing?[13]

Instead of blessing others, some of us fall to pieces when overwhelming life circumstances seem to attack us. Other women are masters of escaping internally, thinking, *If I line my lips perfectly, everyone around me will see my life as perfect.* But Abigail's calm restraint did not in any way overlook the hard, cold truths, or justify sin within her marriage. Friend, with God's help, we can acknowledge issues in all of our relationships head-on—wisely taking action that will bring about healthy change for better tomorrows. But it takes the courage of Abigail to lay the thing that's trying to destroy our lives right on the table, exposing it in the brilliant light of God's love and redeeming power. The powers of darkness don't like the light, my friend. Don't sit in your pain; take action like Abigail.

Dear Lord, how we need the beautiful restraint of Abigail. How we long for an honest-to-goodness courageous countenance where our inner faith becomes external courage. How we want to be courageous women, with impeccable God-timing, so that we can act according to your best leading and trust you with the good results.

No more blaming our husbands, friends, mothers, or our daddies or our dogs for our insecurities. God is about to do a new thing as we courageously discern who He is and come to Him along the dirty little trails of our lives. Do you recognize who God is? Understanding who *He* is really is way more important than knowing who we are. Because when we know who He is, His power will unfold His greater purpose in us, and His wisdom and power will help us in every struggle.

My friend was married to an angry Nabal. Each week she courageously loaded her little ones in the car to go to God's house for worship. Unable to convince her husband to do the right thing, she courageously chose to go. Her obedience positioned and empowered her children to grow up with confidence in the Lord. Today, because my friend didn't throw her faith-shoes in the trash when her walk became too painful, her daughter—now a grown woman with three beautiful children of her own—is following her mother's footsteps, leading *her* family to redeeming love. Friend, things might look impossible but if we will train our child/children in the ways of the Lord, God promises that when they are old, they will not depart from it.[14]

> Stand firm then, with the belt of truth buckled around your waist, with the breastplate of righteousness in place, and with *your feet fitted with the readiness* that comes from the gospel of peace. In addition to all this, take up the shield of faith, with which you can extinguish all the flaming arrows of the evil one. Take the helmet of salvation, and the sword of the Spirit, which is the word of God.
>
> Ephesians 6:14–17 NIV, emphasis added

When we see painful progress, God sees redeeming love at work, and He saw our needs before He ever went to the cross. Remember Palm Sunday? God placed the best He had to offer us on the back of a donkey—Jesus, the gift of salvation, God's one and only Son, the Savior of the world. Our courage-giver, our friend.[15] He sees the cantankerous details of our lives and He carries our burdens. Remember, with every blistering step we take, we are becoming what we will be tomorrow.

Courageously come to your redeemer, Jesus. Come loaded for bear, friend. He *is* the answer to tomorrow's questions. Don't throw your courage away with your uncomfortable shoes. Go! Your better tomorrow awaits you.

COURAGE QUEST

1. How does Abigail's beautiful restraint inspire you to view courage differently? Or to live differently?
2. What impressed you most about Abigail's responses to Nabal's anger?
3. What did you learn from Abigail's actions in the face of impending danger for her family?
4. Courage helped Abigail overcome great obstacles. How can you apply courage to your own life circumstances and be an overcomer?
5. Do you fall to pieces or fall before God asking for direction and wisdom when your life is interrupted by ill-mannered Nabals?

6

Enough

Water must have trickled softly down Bathsheba's beautifully formed body—each water droplet becoming one with the next—as though intentionally tracing her curvaceous waistline, hips, and legs until landing, at last, in a puddle at her feet. *Ahhh* . . . the cleansing stream must have been a welcome reprieve after having experienced her monthly cycle—a time of uncleanliness.[1] As she tilted her head backward, did the soft strokes of her oil-infused sea sponge invite her senses to embrace the stillness of the moment, while also inviting King David to lust?

As Bathsheba continued to bathe, did she open her eyes to see handsome King David[2] standing on the rooftop—just across the way? After taking note of the king's wanting eyes, did Bathsheba sheepishly grab a towel, scream, duck behind a piece of furniture? Was she disheartened to know that her king would stoop to *this* level? Did she feel violated, betrayed, her worth cheapened? We don't really know whether Bathsheba was a victim or a temptress, or if she saw David gazing at all. What is clear is that David wanted her.

> In the spring, at the time when kings go off to war, David sent Joab out with the king's men and the whole Israelite army. They destroyed the Ammonites and besieged Rabbah. But David remained in Jerusalem. One evening David got up from his bed and walked around on the roof of the palace. From the roof he saw a woman bathing. The woman was very beautiful, and David sent someone to find out about her.
>
> 2 Samuel 11:1–3 NIV

Curious King David had many beautiful concubines within the walls of his own palace, enough for a lifetime of sexual pleasure. But in a moment of discontentment, is anything in our lives enough? Doesn't misery cause us to look away from the blessed lives we've been given? Can you think of a time when, from the rooftop of your blessed life, you were unable to embrace simple joys all around you? I can relate.

It's a miserable way to live, friend. When the life we have been given fails to be enough, we sometimes fix our gaze discontentedly toward what we *perceive* as better. As David fixed his gaze on Bathsheba, the beauty within the walls of his own house paled in comparison to his insatiable desire for something more. And in David's case, *someone* more. His discontented lingering led to consuming lust, having eyes for *one* woman only, Bathsheba—Uriah's wife.

> And David sent and inquired about the woman. And the one said: "Is not this Bathsheba, the daughter of Eliam, the wife of Uriah the Hittite?" *So, David sent messengers and took her, and she came to him, and he lay with her.*
>
> 2 Samuel 11:3–4, emphasis added

It Takes Courage to Fight Temptation

Bathsheba's circumstance demanded courage, especially in the aftermath of her encounter with King David. It is a *lack* of courage by this once-stalwart "man after God's own heart"[3] that leads to the devastating consequences requiring Bathsheba to be brave. There are lessons for us in David's failures as well as in Bathsheba's courage to overcome.

Don't you wish we could have been there, talked David down off the ledge of desire? I do. And I'd want to remind him of his past valor, and urge him to gather his own courage to fight this temptation:

> Oh, dear David, what happened to you, my warrior-friend? What a lesson you teach us, that if we don't stand for integrity and rightness of heart we will fall for any lies Satan whispers. Bathsheba doesn't deserve to be the victim of your selfish, sinful desires. She doesn't deserve to pay the price for your idle hands—surely the devil's workshop.[4] This selfish decision will cause so much pain and heartache in the lives of Bathsheba and her husband, Uriah, a dedicated warrior—one of your thirty most trusted men.[5] David, you know God's holy Word: Your battle against temptation began in the garden when Satan convinced Eve that her life was not "enough."[6] Turn your gaze toward God—see His blessings all around you! You've been a warrior since your youth—courageously killing bears and lions.[7] And with only a single stone and a slingshot you defeated a Philistine giant named Goliath.[8] You've fought so hard in times past. Don't compromise your integrity now, my friend. Surely you can fight a little harder in this battle against your discontentment? I hurt for the mistake you are about to make, David, because I know how you previously left behind fear and insecurity for a life of confidence and freedom—leading others to do the same. Think about the fear and insecurity you will cause Bathsheba and how this will affect her life.

But King David had his mind made up. He would have Bathsheba, no matter what or who stood in his way. David accepted the lie of the enemy that Bathsheba was the "more" he must have. With reports of sexual assaults on college and university campuses on the rise, the all-too-common theme of Bathsheba's story breaks my heart. I know many young women who have been the victim of a man's sinful, selfish desires.

Scripture doesn't tell us if Bathsheba was tempted by David's poetic ways or if she wanted to resist his pursuit. I certainly don't want to add to or water down what Scripture has to say about Bathsheba and David's escapade. But temptation can cut both ways, and I do meet many women who candidly share about their temptation to gaze at other men, whether fantasizing about having more romance in their lives or simply indulging in lustful thinking caused by living in a world where it seems anything is okay as long as it feels good.

Pointing the finger of blame is not my intent. My hope is that we will courageously think about a time in our lives when we became bored, restless—looking for more. I think this sums up Bathsheba's plight: She was at the mercy of a bored king who had it all and still longed for more

My friend Ann was tempted to gaze and linger in want for more than her life. After being married for almost twenty years, with four beautiful children of her own, Ann received the news that her first love had lost his wife in a tragic accident and was now a bachelor. When Ann reached out to offer her condolences, memories came flooding back. At first, Ann simply gazed, the old, familiar, lovin' feelings tugging at her heart. He was still as kind as ever and he made Ann feel beautiful, loved, and respected. Then, Ann lingered—unable to stop thinking about him. Soon, she acted on her feelings, which turned into an emotional affair.

Her first love was everything her husband was not. Her husband was unemotional and disconnected, never complimenting her and failing to consider her in thoughtful ways. Everything about her first love, however, made her feel alive, special, complete—that she was enough. As Ann continued to gaze into her past, discontentment grew. The sin of her emotional affair began causing anxiety and fear. With tears filling her eyes, Ann shared with me, saying, "Every time I thought of leaving, I would think of how my children would suffer, and I couldn't bear the thought—no matter how tempting."

Ann went into spiritual battle, calling on the power of God that was in her DNA. She courageously turned her gaze away from the temptation, and toward the One who had created her in His image, the One who knew the depth of every emotion. Sometime later, Ann said, "LaTan, people need to realize the power of falling on their knees, acknowledging the power of God to bring freedom." And that's exactly what Ann did. She dropped to her knees and poured it all out, courageously confessing to God:

"Lord, take my heart and change it. Lord, take these feelings away. I know this will destroy my family." As tears rolled down Ann's cheeks, she said, "LaTan, God answered that prayer. And just last night, my husband and I were on a date and I told him, 'I really like you. I really enjoy spending time with you. You are so much fun to be with.' God is at work healing our marriage. Now, if I turn music on that reminds me of my first love, I turn it off."

Thankfully, Ann took God up on His promise in 1 Corinthians 10:13 to offer her a way of escape from temptation. Will you do the same, friend? Rather than destroy her family, Ann turned her gaze to the One who is enough. It takes courage to keep fighting the good fight when our flesh is tempted to choose comfort and compromise over confidence in the One who offers us tools for positive change and the courage to face the truth.

Courage to Face Truth

> Then she returned to her house. And the woman conceived, and she sent and told David, "I am pregnant."
>
> 2 Samuel 11:4–5

Did Bathsheba feel objectified and defiled? I would have! Imagine the feelings of shame, the fear, the anxiety. Imagine the courage it would have taken to return to her home and not simply flee after such an ordeal. Facing our stressful circumstances is not for sissies. And Bathsheba had to face her situation, look it square in the face and feel the panic of realizing she had conceived a child by the king her husband had faithfully served.

Bathsheba had not had a choice in honoring the king's command, and now she had no choice but to carry evidence of David's sin inside her body for the world to see. Panic. Both she and King David must have felt it. How would they smooth out this mess?

This reminds me of a time in my childhood when my mother had bought a container of Cool Whip and a box of vanilla wafer cookies. She told me about her plans to make banana pudding for Sunday's lunch and said not to open them. Well, I stood with the refrigerator door open and gazed at the Cool Whip. Soon, my lingering turned to temptation—*imagining* what it would taste like wasn't good enough for me. Gazing didn't satisfy me. And lingering only made my cravings stronger. None of these was enough.

Before I knew it, my eight-year-old fingers were busily dipping vanilla wafers into the Cool Whip, like potato chips and dip. For the first few dives into the creamy whip, I experienced the ultimate sense of satisfaction—taking as much as I wanted and enjoying every moment. But I wasn't satisfied for long because our cravings for wrongdoing have a way of turning sour, quickly.

You'd think we'd remember this in the next round of temptations that come our way, huh? Yet, our memories are too short for our own good. And my short-lived memories of past wrongdoing had led me to this big problem: The Cool Whip and the vanilla wafers were *not* my property. I had no right to open them or to indulge myself in them; they belonged to my mother.

As panic set in, I desperately devised a plan to cover up the wrong I'd done: I used a round-edged utensil and very carefully tried to smooth over the top of the Cool Whip; I even tried to create the little swirl in the center, convincing myself that no one would ever know about my little escapade. But, of course, my sins found me out, and I was in big trouble.

I was a child. King David was not. But he was acting like a child who was determined to have his way—and poor Bathsheba would pay the price for his rebellion.

In the same way that I took my mother's property, King David took Uriah's property—Bathsheba—as his own and indulged himself to satisfy a momentary pleasure. And like me, he tried to smooth over his sin afterward, which we can read about in 2 Samuel 11:6–25.

King David's desperate plan was to send word for Uriah to come home from battle. And when Uriah arrived, David tried to act like nothing had happened—casually asking Uriah how the war was going. Then David said to Uriah, "Go down to your house and wash your feet" (v. 8). He even sent a present to Uriah. Trying to smooth his sin over a bit more, King David encouraged Uriah to sleep with his wife, in hopes of making Uriah think Bathsheba had conceived *his* child. But Uriah, being a man of integrity, would not go home and he would not sleep with Bathsheba, telling the king:

> "The ark and Israel and Judah dwell in booths, and my lord Joab and the servants of my lord are camping in the open field.

> Shall I then go to my house, to eat and to drink and to lie with my wife?"
>
> 2 Samuel 11:11

And David took his invisible butter knife and created another swirl in his Cool Whip—convincing Uriah to stay in Jerusalem for two days. Uriah submits to King David and joins him for a meal, and David gets Uriah drunk—thinking he would surely go to Bathsheba, his wife, and lie with her. But humble, courageous Uriah went out to lie on his couch with the servants, and didn't go to his house—talk about integrity of heart! Now King David was even more desperate to smooth over his sinful indulgence and he sent a letter by Uriah to Joab, the commander in battle, telling him to place Uriah in the forefront of the hardest fighting, and then draw back from him so he would be killed.

No amount of smoothing things over would fix the problem.

Bathsheba belonged to her husband, Uriah—a brave and loyal soldier who was fully focused on battle. Confessing would have been the right thing for King David to do; but he lacked the courage to walk in the freedom that truth and confession bring to us. And no swirls would cover up the sinful liberties David had taken with Bathsheba.

> But the thing that David had done displeased the Lord.
>
> 2 Samuel 11:27

And God is not pleased with our selfish, sinful motives either. He wants you and me to live confidently, experiencing spiritual freedom. Only by remembering the power residing inside of us can we be victorious over our indulgent momentary sins. Otherwise, we make God into a pint-sized Savior who fits in our purses. And we try to use His power as we see fit, for our convenience. Only by keeping a gaze of wonder on how *big* God truly is can we leave behind our fearful life of insecurity to face our temptations courageously, knowing God has made a way of escape.

> No temptation has overtaken you that is not common to man. God is faithful, and he will not let you be tempted beyond your ability, but with the temptation he will also provide the way of escape, that you may be able to endure it.
>
> 1 Corinthians 10:13

And so . . . we close the refrigerator door (things tempting us to live discontentedly) and gaze toward our own family and the blessings inside our own house, change the channel on the television instead of lingering at inappropriate images. And we stop, drop, and pray—right in the middle of the most tempting of days. Because courageous women fight for their tomorrows. And consider how every choice affects the innocent ones in our lives too.

Courage Helps Us Face Death

Hot tears fell down Bathsheba's beautiful face after hearing the news of her husband's death.[9] Did she feel love for her husband, Uriah, or long for his loving arms to hold her once more? Scripture doesn't tell us if she and Uriah shared a mutually passionate, loving relationship. But since it does tell us that Bathsheba lamented over Uriah's death, I think it's safe to say that Uriah had won her heart with his kind and respectful ways and most likely never made her feel objectified. Uriah was a man who thought of others. He refused to rush in, sleep with Bathsheba, indulge himself during battle while his friends and comrades were enduring miserable conditions. And his thoughtful integrity must have spilled over into the private places of his life—to his wife, Bathsheba.

After Bathsheba's mourning was over, King David brought her to his house to become his wife.[10] She had already experienced so much sadness and loss, and would also experience the tragic death of the child she had conceived with King David.[11]

My own mother and many of my dear friends can relate to Bathsheba's heartache at the loss of a child. These women have expressed to me the abundant amounts of courage they needed to continue breathing, to go on living, after experiencing so much pain and loss.

Bathsheba's likely emotional state can be best summed up by listing the quick succession of major life stressors she faced: being taken by David, an unplanned pregnancy, her husband's murder, the loss of a child.

Perhaps you have lost a child and are feeling compassion for Bathsheba. The eventual outcome of painful loss is that it allows us to comfort others in a very deep and personal way, understanding when others can't. But if you aren't at a place emotionally to even think about comforting others, allow God to comfort you, friend. Fix your gaze on Jesus. Linger and indulge yourself by diving into the sweetness of His holy Word—be sure to double dip!

You are God's property, His beautiful love. And His holy Word is His love letter to you. God will give you the strength you need to face even your most painful battles, and He is faithfully fighting against your fear, anxiety, and hopelessness. He's fighting alongside you for your marriage, your family, and for everything you deal with as a woman. He wants you to recognize that He is enough, because when you do you will know that you are enough too. And the temptation to gaze at the lives of others and wish for more will diminish.

Courage to Be Content

When God is no longer enough, nothing will ever be enough, my friend.

Sure, God had been enough for David in times past. But David couldn't ride on yesterday's victories, and neither can we. Each day presents a different temptation. A different kind of struggle. Whether we are potty training our toddlers and losing our tempers, or staring down our anxious, aging selves in the mirror. God will be enough for our wanting hearts and our broken-down bodies. He is our yesterday, our today, and our forever.

Remember, friend, we don't wrestle against flesh and blood, "but against the rulers, against the authorities, against the cosmic powers over this present darkness, against the spiritual forces of evil in the heavenly places" (Ephesians 6:12).

There's no way I can truly know what you are thinking as you read this, but, since I interact with lots of women, I can safely guess some of you are thinking, *LaTan, you have no idea! My husband hasn't touched me in six months. We look happy from the outside looking in—but passion? Ha! What a joke! If a king—or a pauper, for that matter—looked at me with wanting eyes about now, well . . .*

My friend, I think Bathsheba would tell you not to objectify yourself. Keep your gaze on God. Don't allow the empty void you feel to cause you to enjoy attention from other men. Fill your life with more of God and as you do your love cup will be so full you'll have no room for an unworthy man to pour into you. And like my friend Ann, when life feels like it's not enough—pray like you've never prayed so you can experience God's enough like you never have. I think our courage is best measured by our ability to do the right thing when everything in our flesh wants to do wrong. Ann passed her test. We can too!

Although King David failed his test and gave in to temptation, causing a long list of sins to follow, God would show mercy and provide some restoration. God would honor Bathsheba and David with a second son, Solomon, who would succeed King David on the throne and become the wisest man ever to have lived.[12]

Finding Courage to Accept the Redeeming Power of God

Despite how defiled Bathsheba might have been when King David took her, the next time he came to Bathsheba he would do so not as the thoughtless adulterer but as a comforting husband. God would also bless Bathsheba by allowing her to have a close and intimate relationship with her son. While his father, David, might have disrespected Bathsheba in the beginning, God would redeem even that, by filling her son, King Solomon, with a deep love and respect put on display for his mother seen in 1 Kings 2:19. King Solomon stood to meet his mother, Bathsheba, bowing down to her. Oh, friend, how I love the redeeming sweetness of God to allow us to see firsthand the respect Bathsheba is shown from this son of David. And how beautiful it is that God would allow us to read how King Solomon had a seat brought into his throne room especially for his mother—positioning Bathsheba at his right hand, making her a treasured advisor.

It also takes courage to parent with confidence when the voices of guilt and shame ask: Who do you think you are to steer a child toward integrity-based living? You've made all the mistakes in the world and your child-rearing is fruitless! Friend, don't listen to these voices of condemnation. You can parent confidently, as I believe Bathsheba must have, knowing God can redeem all things and will use our weaknesses to help us parent with transparency and power. Don't shrink back from holding God's standard just because you failed to meet it once upon a time.

It takes courage to say no to ourselves when sin wants us to give in. And it takes courage to recognize God as a filling agent for the empty recesses of our broken hearts when our husbands have gone astray. It takes spiritual maturity for us not to want simply to prove we can still captivate another man's heart. Friend, receiving no attention is better than capturing the wrong attention. And we'd all be wise to learn from Bathsheba and David that no sin ever goes undiscovered. Every sinful wrong will be exposed, in time.[13] I'm so thankful that while we were yet sinners, Jesus died for us.[14]

Imagine the kind of courage it must have required for Bathsheba to refuse to allow David's sinful actions to ruin her life. Even when we feel we are the victims in any given circumstance, it takes courage to take a good, hard look at the situation and let go of the shame, the guilt, the voices of condemnation, so that true healing can come. And sometimes courage will help us own our part of the fault, if there is any to be owned. Courage will help us stand confidently, knowing that although we were wronged, hurt, abused, and perhaps even abandoned, we are more than conquerors through the One who created us. Even if we have instigated the trouble at hand, God is bigger than our sins and failure.

Friend, God will use the worst parts of our stories, if we will let Him. Will you let Him? God used the worst part of Bathsheba's story to show His redeeming love. Through unwise sinners He would birth the wisest man, King Solomon.[15] I think Bathsheba's challenge for us all is to not allow one person's sin to ruin our entire lives, or our future influence. To keep believing that no matter what happened in our yesterdays, tomorrow will be better *because* it happened. God wastes nothing, and He makes all things possible.[16] He is merciful and gracious, slow to anger, and abounding in steadfast love and faithfulness.[17]

Do you see courage coming as you refocus your heart toward holy living? I do! Run like mad from any temptation that threatens to overcome you. You *are* an overcomer, my precious warrior-friend. Say this aloud:

I am a wise woman of the Word. I am courageously focused on the battles before me. I acknowledge that God is enough! And because He is enough, I am enough. My past does not define me. My children will become wiser, stronger, and more courageous, day by day, as I courageously live transparently, leading them to the heart of God by choosing courage over fear and anxiety, right over wrong, integrity over evil.

Do you think a new wisdom was birthed in Bathsheba and King David as they held their son Solomon in their arms? I do. The past has a beautiful way of sanding our sinful, rough edges off while unveiling our real inner beauty. Our past mistakes can birth new wisdom in us as well. Don't run, hide, or compromise. Jesus, the One who will never exploit, defile, or use you, is calling you to come into His chamber, wanting deeper intimacy. He adores every part of you, and He delights in gazing upon your beauty. In Him, *you* are enough!

COURAGE QUEST

1. Have you ever been victimized by someone you respected greatly?
2. Courage can help us to have a better attitude or act courageously when our circumstances demand it. Courage can help us to speak up when we need to and keep quiet when

wisdom tells us that's best. How has courage helped you to live victoriously, even when you have been wronged?

3. Is God "enough" to captivate your gaze when you are mistreated, or are you held hostage by the something or someone from your past?
4. Perhaps you have been wounded by someone in a different way than sexually and are struggling to live courageously beyond the hurt. Has the pain caused you to retreat in fear of future rejection? Do you feel alone and isolated?
5. It takes courage to forgive someone who has caused us great pain. Is there someone you need to forgive? Sometimes the most powerful gift we can give to ourselves is the gift of forgiveness, and sometimes we need to forgive ourselves before forgiving others. Pray the following prayer with a sincere heart:

Father, this pain has held me captive for so long. I want to be set free. Give me the courage to forgive myself, letting go of guilt and shame. Help me to give and receive love without fears and insecurities blocking my way. Forgive me for my unforgiving heart toward others. And help me to forgive ______________, right now, so that I can let go of the disappointment and expectations I have placed on others. No circumstance or person is my God. You are my God. Help me grab hold of the truth that You are enough for all of my days. Amen.

Come Empty, Leave Full

> So Jesus, wearied as he was from his journey, was sitting beside the well. It was about the sixth hour.
>
> John 4:6

The Samaritan woman must have walked with intent—her empty water jug resting firmly atop her head, and her heart full of sin. With quick, even strides did her strong legs press hard into the earth beneath her? Did she wish to be invisible—keeping her eyes to the ground—to avoid the glares of condemnation? Or did she chuckle inwardly, amused by her own sarcastic thoughts?

The way these people are scattering about, you'd think I have leprosy!

The women's pointing fingers and hands cupped to the sides of their mouths said it all. Did they think she deserved their whispers of condemnation? Did her own thoughts condemn her to greater shame?

Were the noisy, swarming women without sin? Is any one of us without sin? Wasn't it better to be completely empty in spirit than to be filled with gossip?[1] Did they think her shameful life choices weighed heavier on their religious morality scale? Was this how they justified turning their noses in the air as she walked past, as though catching a whiff of the stench of her lifestyle?

Is this what we would have done to the Samaritan woman?

These tormenting mind games might have been the reason why the Samaritan woman came to Jacob's well in the midday heat—purposefully avoiding the gawking group of women who'd gather later in the day when it was cooler. How she must have detested their prideful enjoyment of mocking others. Did focusing on her imperfections make them feel better about themselves?

The conflicts between Jews and Samaritans had gone on for years, with ethnic hatred dividing the two. And as a lower-class, promiscuous Samaritan woman, she would have been accustomed to poor treatment from men and women alike. But she must have felt the pain of rejection cutting into the core of her being—or would she have been able to feel at all, if she was as emotionally downcast and as empty as her clay water jar?

Courage to Stay and Engage

Can you see her in your mind, carefully lifting the water jug from her head and placing it on the ground next to Jacob's well? With strong arms and quick hands—working hard to ignore the man she'd only caught a tiny glimpse of? *Why is He sitting on the other side of the well? And what must He want from me?*

Her thoughts were interrupted by a voice: "Give me a drink."[2] Surely she was hallucinating. Perhaps because of the heat of the midday sun?

How could she not have been stunned, wondering, *What could possibly have motivated this man to speak to a despised half-breed Samaritan woman, and in public no less?* No respectable Jewish man would take the risk of talking to any woman in public—especially a woman like her.[3] If her eyes hadn't been playing tricks, her ears surely were. Had He really asked *her* for a drink of water? She'd been asked to give men a lot of things in her lifetime, but I'm guessing a drink of water wasn't the usual request.

How could she have perceived that what He had asked for *He was*—Living Water. And that she would soon experience grace, perhaps for the first time in her life. If she had known, she might have danced her way to the well. No matter how she'd wanted to avoid Him, she could not dismiss the gentle tone of Jesus' voice. Perhaps no man had ever spoken to her so tenderly.

Did she clear her throat—keeping her voice equally as soft?

> "How is it that you, a Jew, ask for a drink from me, a woman of Samaria?" (For Jews have no dealings with Samaritans.)
>
> John 4:9

Was He there to mock her? To trick her in some way? This might have been her experience with other men, so why would she trust the motives of this man, Jesus? How could He possibly be any different from the others who had treated her so disrespectfully?

If by some chance she'd questioned these things, one look in His eyes might put her heart at rest:

> "If you knew the gift of God, and who it is that is saying to you, 'Give me a drink,' you would have asked him, and he would have given you living water."
>
> John 4:10

> The woman said to him, "Sir, you have nothing to draw water with, and the well is deep. Where do you get that living water? Are you greater than our father Jacob? He gave us the well and drank from it himself, as did his sons and his livestock." Jesus said to her, "Everyone who drinks of this water will be thirsty again, but whoever drinks of the water that I will give him will never be thirsty again. The water that I will give him will become in him a spring of water welling up to eternal life." The woman said to him, "Sir, give me this water, so that I will not be thirsty or have to come here to draw water." Jesus said to her, "Go, call your husband and come here." The woman answered him, "I have no husband." Jesus said to her, "You are right in saying, 'I have no husband'; *for you have had five husbands, and the one you now have is not your husband.*"
>
> John 4:11–18, emphasis added

Did she drop her water jar to the ground, stunned by the words Jesus had spoken? How did this perfect stranger know everything she'd ever done? The truth of her life came to the surface, exposing every lie—but with compassion, not the condemnation she had been subjected to by others. Condemnation she was familiar with—compassion, not so much. The more Jesus spoke, the more the muddy waters of her shame ran clear.

How could she not have been mesmerized by this Jewish man with His mysterious ability to dive into the depths of her dry soul, without laying a hand on her? Even if she'd felt the urge to run away, His powerful, compassionate presence gave her courage to stay—drawing her in—near His deep well, like her empty jar ready to be filled.

> "Sir, I perceive that you are a prophet. Our fathers worshiped on this mountain, but you say that in Jerusalem is the place where people ought to worship."
>
> John 4:19

As Jesus' holy eyes penetrated the muddy waters of her soul, did she feel the need to steer Him in a direction that would validate her worth? *My family has a history of being faithful worshipers. I don't know who you are, but I think you are a prophet; how else can you see the colorful stories within me? I'm not so bad, really. I might look like a low-life sinner, but, my family had faith. In fact, some of the men in my family worshiped on a mountain, in the high places. They weren't ashamed to let others know they believed in God.*

Or, perhaps she wanted to remind this Jew that He shouldn't talk to her for more reasons than one. Aside from the fact that men didn't even speak to their wives in public, Jews wouldn't willingly speak to Samaritans either. The Jews and Samaritans had a history of hostilities and were longtime religious competitors, having built rival temples on Mount Gerizim.[4] The Samaritan woman might have been rejected by society, but she was graciously received by Jesus; I think it's important to note that His longest one-on-one conversation recorded was with this disreputable lady.[5]

Courage to Experience Greater Intimacy

Jesus wanted the woman at the well to experience a greater intimacy with God than her ancestors did. Do you believe He wants the same for you and me? I think He waited by the well, perfect gentleman of a savior that He is, not to force himself upon her, like other men might have, but to show her the way to God's heart. No racial, cultural, or religious barriers would divide His heart away from hers. Jesus wanted her to experience a relationship with God the Father. He *was* the way to God's heart, and her ultimate freedom would come through Him. She could not ride on the religious rituals of times past. And neither can we, friend.

The relationship my grandparents had with the Lord isn't *my* relationship. And my sins aren't erased because of the good deeds my family did in times past. The Samaritan woman would have to experience Jesus for herself. Her advantage was living in a time when Jesus had come to save the world from sin and shame. How timely and how on point His coming was. Her ancestors had to offer sacrifices, but she was experiencing God personified, Jesus Christ, the lamb that would soon be slain for her sin, her shame.

How wonderful for the Samaritan woman and for a woman like me—sinful as we are. And how wonderful for a woman like you, too, friend. To live in a time when we can freely approach Jesus at the wells of our lives. He's waiting for us to come to Him. And when we come, He lovingly receives us, just as we are. He offered the woman at the well an opportunity to begin a new faith legacy, greater than her ancestors'. But how could she grasp His wanting to fill her with living water—to never thirst again? What did that mean?

Never having to come back to the well again sounded too good to be true. Drawing from the well was a weekly and sometimes daily routine and was exhausting, back-breaking work. It was a job she'd gladly retire from. But there were people, animals, and crops depending on her coming to Jacob's well. By this point, her curiosity about the gift Jesus promised must have been at an all-time high—higher than the mountain her ancestors had worshiped on.

The gift had everything to do with His filling her with new life—gifting her with all that He was: love, mercy, and grace that would wash away her sin. Her void would be filled to the brim with His spirit, with no empty spaces for the muddy waters of her sinful life to pour in again.

It must have taken some pretty big courage to listen to a stranger recount her sinful past. As she thought about all the things Jesus knew about her, and how He still treated her with dignity, she must have been moved beyond words. Or perhaps her sin had become such a familiar part of her life that it didn't seem like sin at all. Perhaps she didn't realize the person she was becoming.

Do you ever feel like the person you are today snuck up behind you and took you by surprise? Life has a way of pouring into us toxic solutions we accept as truth. And I think we don't realize the dangers of what we are capable of becoming, little by little, day by day as the world around us influences our beliefs. We live in a culture where there are no wrongs—as long as what we are experiencing feels good. But as we discussed in chapter 6, every choice made today affects our tomorrows. Little compromises become big ones and before we know it, we've moved off the mountain we once worshiped on into a muddy pit of sinful living. The Samaritan woman's sins had stripped her of more than social standing, including her integrity, her reputation, her family legacy, and her ability to feel love, receive love, and express love. Jesus wanted her to come empty and leave filled with His Spirit.

When my son left for college, he took most everything he owned with him. His room was empty and our voices echoed off the walls. But when the room was filled up again, sound was absorbed, and the echo didn't exist. I think the gift of the life-giving waters Jesus offered the Samaritan woman had the power to fill her up and stop the echoing voices of those who thrived on devaluing her. She was thirsty for something but couldn't find it. And each lover left her feeling even more empty inside.

Have you tried to satisfy your empty soul's thirst with temporary loves? Maybe the love of your life is your job, or your pride, perhaps money or your need for approval from others? Think about the different things you have sought to fill your empty life with. For the Samaritan woman, it was five men, with a sixth in the works.

What six things do you give more physical energy and more time to than growing a loving relationship of faith in Christ? It takes courage to listen to Jesus, the Voice of Truth, as He lovingly calls us away from toxic living. The Samaritan woman's life was poisonous. But as Jesus spoke, He poured out truth that would call out sin and call her into a healthier way of living.

Do you like the woman you've become, friend? If not, it's never too late to change. Perhaps you want to change but feel as though you can't accept the gift of God because you have nothing to give? It's okay! Jesus expected nothing but gave His all to the Samaritan woman, and He has given His all for you and me too. But when I pray, "Lord, I want *all* that you are," I'm quickly reminded that I will never be able to grasp all that He is until I meet Him face-to-face in heaven someday.

Last week while in Canada, I visited Niagara Falls and watched in amazement as large tourist boats approached the falls. The powerful force of water crashing all around made them look so tiny. And my problems felt small and insignificant too, as I thought about how the power of the Niagara pales in comparison to all God truly is. I wondered if the Samaritan woman felt the same sense of awe as she experienced the rushing power of heaven's truth spoken over her empty life. When Jesus asked her for a drink, He wanted her to recognize and experience the rushing power inside of Him. She had all the water needed to wash clothes, and enough to replenish herself physically. But she needed *all* that Jesus was to fill her empty soul. And so do we.

Do you feel His truth pouring over you as you read about the Samaritan woman? Remember when Jesus told her to "Go, call your husband and come here"? He was basically telling her, "Bring the things you have vainly tried to fill your empty void with, and while you are at it, bring me all the guilt, shame, and disgrace."

As I write this, Jesus meets me by the well—my black leather chair that sits in my kitchen. It's where I come to lower my emptiness into the deep waters of His Spirit each morning. In the same way the power of the Niagara provides electricity for millions of households, the Holy Spirit powers my life with light—exposing my sin—helping me walk in true freedom. The woman at the well couldn't be truly filled until she freed up some space, allowing Jesus to bear her sin and fill her with contentment and love.

As Jesus asked the Samaritan woman to bring her husbands to Him, I sense Him asking me:

"Where are the things that give you self-esteem?"

"Where is your worry?"

"Where is your pride?"

"Where is your wayward child?"

"Where is your anger?"

"Where is your shame?"

"Where is your gossip?"

"Where is your sadness?"

"Go, call them to come here, LaTan. I'm sitting by the well of your life, eager for you to bring anything and everything that drains you dry. Bring your emptiness and experience my fullness.[6] *Then I can move in you with a power you could never experience otherwise."*

Jesus wanted the Samaritan woman to go call her husbands, to also acknowledge the things she'd been vainly filling her life with. Her sins had dehydrated her soul, friend. Jesus wanted her to confess guilt and shame so He could fill her up with His spirit—life-giving, cleansing waters. If she had refused Jesus, she would have missed out on the best gift of her life—the gift of eternal life.

Thankfully, on that day at the well, when God's son, Jesus, offered all that He was, she accepted it. Jesus came to Jacob's well for the same reason He had come into the world:

> To proclaim the year of the Lord's favor,
> and the day of vengeance of our God;
> to comfort all who mourn;
> to grant to those who mourn in Zion—
> to give them a beautiful headdress instead of ashes,
> the oil of gladness instead of mourning,
> the garment of praise instead of a faint spirit;
> that they may be called oaks of righteousness,
> the planting of the Lord, that he may be glorified.
> They shall build up the ancient ruins;
> they shall raise up the former devastations;
> they shall repair the ruined cities,
> the devastations of many generations.
>
> Isaiah 61:2–4

Courage to Receive God's Lavish Love

The Samaritan woman's poor, dry soul was filled to the brim with life-giving waters of His spirit. Can you see her? Life-giving, cleansing waters infused with truth and grace flooding every cracked crevice of her empty, barren past? The Samaritan woman heard the truth of the gospel, felt it, received it, and was changed from the inside out. And that's what Jesus will do for thirsty women like me and you too.

No man had ever gifted her so. It was a gift with no strings attached. Jesus was not just any face, He was *the* face of grace, the courage-giver who met her at the well, right in the middle of her promiscuous life. And He meets you and me right in the middle of our dehydrated lives too. Lavishing us with His love, mercy, and grace. But it takes courage to receive all that He is, to allow the cleansing waters to refresh, restore, renew our dry souls.

God set His grace into motion when He sent His son, Jesus, our perfect gift of salvation. How could the woman at the well have known that Jesus came to *love* her to truth? Her idea of love must have been terribly distorted, with so many men taking more and more of her identity with each encounter. But this man, Jesus, wanted nothing from her. He came to give. He came for people like us: the downcast, the lowly, the prostitutes, murderers, and thieves, the wives who have been betrayed, the ones whose dreams have been dashed, whose high hopes have been drowned in deep wells of past regret, the women on food stamps, the women with big, abundant bank accounts and poor love accounts, those striving to impress—chasing after affirmation—drinking from the tainted wells of people who use and abuse them.

But sometimes we become comfortable living our sinful lives. And sometimes it seems we just don't know any better—until courage calls us to acknowledge the better way. Jesus, the courage-giver, was calling the Samaritan woman to acknowledge that what He had to offer her was way better than what she'd been drawing out of the well of her life. She might have a tainted past—trapped in a riptide of failed relationships—but courage was calling her to resist the current.

When my daughter was a teenager, she went on a beach trip with the youth group. She waded casually out into the ocean and was sucked under by a riptide. Unable to resist the current, she quickly found herself spinning out of control underneath the salty waters of the Atlantic Ocean. As the strong undercurrent continued to drag her down the beach, and farther away from the group, she could only hear the loud sound of the water squishing around her. In her panic, she remembered having watched a documentary about the dangers of riptides. It said if you are caught in one to dig deep into the sand when you come to the bottom, and crawl toward the shore. When she was finally able to stand on her feet, she walked with trembling knees out of the same salty waters that had pulled her under minutes before. But the sad part was, no one even saw her go under or noticed her struggle.

I think that's what happened to the Samaritan woman. The strong undercurrent of poor life choices had sucked her down—spinning her completely out of control—the swishing noise of her sinful cycle dragging her further and further away from God's best. And most likely, no one noticed her struggle until the courage-giver, Jesus, met her at the well.

What about you? Are you ready to be free of whatever it is that's dragging you down and away from God? Do you feel you can only hear the sound of whatever riptide you are caught in? Come crawling. Listen for the swishing sound of courage calling you to grab hold of Jesus, your solid place. When no one notices that you are drowning, Jesus does. How wonderful it is to know that the magnificent power of heaven has made *you* His main priority. Do you feel it?

The Samaritan woman did.

> "Come, see a man who told me all that I ever did. Can this be the Christ?"
>
> John 4:29

A new day had dawned in the Samaritan woman's life. As new life filled every fiber of her being, confidence followed, giving her the courage to run through the streets fearlessly confessing all the truth of what Jesus had spoken to her—the same streets where she had once walked in shame, she now ran in freedom. She would worship Jesus in spirit and in truth, courageously proclaiming His name. Not on a mountain in a far-off distant remote place, but up close and personal. And she would shout her faith out loud like her ancestors had done all those years ago. This should give us all hope, knowing that the seeds we've faithfully sown in the lives of our family will spring forth when the waters of God's spirit touch them, in the right place, at the right time.

> Many Samaritans from that town believed in him because of the woman's testimony, "He told me all that I ever did." So when the Samaritans came to him, they asked him to stay with them, and he stayed there two days. And many more believed because of his word. They said to the woman, "It is no longer because of what you said that we believe, for we have heard for ourselves, and we know that this is indeed the Savior of the world."
>
> John 4:39–42

Even when life pulls the plug, leaving us drained, we can be joyful knowing Jesus doesn't own an empty well. The gift of His supply is endless.

So, will you come to the well? Come, with your empty water jar. Come frazzled, cracked, chipped, broken. Courageously come without shrinking back in fear. Jesus sees you, and He loves you—just as you are. Come empty, leave full!

> "Let anyone who is thirsty come to me and drink. Whoever believes in me, as Scripture has said, rivers of living water will flow from within them."
>
> John 7:37–38 NIV

COURAGE QUEST

1. Do you need courage to receive God's lavish love?
2. Can you remember a time when you came to God empty and left your prayer time full of the living water He provided you?
3. How would you have felt if you were the Samaritan woman?
4. It took courage for the Samaritan woman to engage with Jesus, especially after He told her He knew everything she had ever done. Does your personal shame hinder you from conversing with Jesus in prayer? He sees the core of your being and loves you still.
5. Has life left you spiritually dehydrated? Do you feel the need to come to the well? Ask Jesus to give you the water that will help satisfy your dry and thirsty soul. What do you need the Spirit of God to wash away—a bad memory, past guilt and shame, an unbearable regret, a sin you are trapped in currently? Remember, friend, Jesus waited for the Samaritan woman to approach the well, and He is waiting for you to come to Him also.

8

Birthing Courage

"Greetings, oh favored one, the Lord is with you!"[1] Gabriel's words had been dominating and powerful—yet soothing to Mary's soul. Years after Mary had been chosen as Jesus' mother, she must have remembered how her eyes had squinted—struggling to adjust to Gabriel's brilliant light filling the room:

> And the angel said to her, "Do not be afraid, Mary, for you have found favor with God. And behold, you will conceive in your womb and bear a son, and you shall call his name Jesus. He will be great and will be called the Son of the Most High. And the Lord God will give to him the throne of his father David, and he will reign over the house of Jacob forever, and of his kingdom there will be no end."
>
> Luke 1:30–33

How small Mary must have felt as Gabriel's magnificent presence enlightened and filled her with God's higher truth.

Gabriel's words had been sure and direct—leaving Mary with questions, including:

> "How will this be, since I am a virgin?"
>
> Luke 1:34

Gabriel's answer came to her troubled heart as quickly as he'd appeared to her.

> "The Holy Spirit will come upon you, and the power of the Most High will overshadow you; therefore the child to be born will be called holy—the Son of God."
>
> v. 35

Perhaps Mary's innocence of youth was a gift. If she had known the painful days ahead of her, she might have fallen facedown, trembling in fear.

Did she feel shock or honor as Gabriel finished his message? Wasn't it every Jewish girl's dream to have a son? And to think His name would be great? *Awesome! I'll take that, God!* Most of us would confess to wanting our children to be important little people who grow up to be important big adults, right? And . . . He would reign, rule, and have a kingdom that would never end? *Whoa! God, you are talking this mother's love language. I have two sons, and I want them to reign and rule as kings! Yes, Lord, sign me up!*

Didn't every Jewish girl want to experience God's blessings for obedience on her life? *Blessings that would overtake her: in the city and in the field, in the fruit of her womb, the fruit of the ground, fruit of her cattle, increase of her herds, blessed baskets and kneading bowls, blessed in her coming and her going, her enemies would be defeated before her—coming out against her one way and fleeing before her seven ways, blessings on her personally, blessings on her barns and all she would undertake, blessings in the land God would give.*[2]

Such an honor would only come from a life surrendered to God. Everything Gabriel had said had been foretold. God had promised His people in Deuteronomy that when others saw their obedience to God they would be afraid of them. Didn't every Jewish girl want to live a life of obedience with the promise of God? *The Lord would open His good treasury—the heavens—to give rain on her land in due season, and bless the work of her hands; she would lend to many nations but borrow from none; the Lord would make her the head and not the tail; and she would go up and not down, if she obeyed the commandments of the Lord her God.*[3]

Did Mary gasp at the thought of experiencing the fullness of God's blessing? How must she have felt to know she would carry the fullness of God personified *literally* inside her womb? The One who would break off all gender prejudice, racial prejudice, cultural prejudice. The One whose free gift would be for all—men, women, red, yellow, black, or white. Can you imagine being in Mary's position? Such a thought is not to be taken lightly. Surely Mary knew Gabriel's presence was of supreme importance. And if the message he'd already given her wasn't enough news for the day, Gabriel had more:

> "And behold, your relative Elizabeth in her old age has also conceived a son, and this is the sixth month with her who was called barren. For nothing will be impossible with God."
>
> Luke 1:36–37

God had surely done the impossible: Elizabeth was well past birthing years, and Mary so young and a virgin. How wonderful of God to bless Elizabeth. How painful it would have been telling childless Elizabeth the news that she had been chosen to carry the Savior of the world—at such a young age—while Elizabeth had waited for years to conceive. But God was ahead of Mary every step of the way, carving through impossible fears and intimidations—setting the stage for Mary to courageously embrace the miraculous.

> "Behold, I am the servant of the Lord; let it be to me according to your word."
>
> Luke 1:38

Did her bold response to Gabriel feel like an out-of-body experience? Was courage birthed right then and there as she embraced, with confidence, God's purposed positioning in her life—to become the mother of Jesus, the savior of the world? Was it as though heaven itself had spoken courageously *for her*?

Heaven would smooth things over with her fiancé, Joseph, sending an angel in a dream, after he realized she was pregnant and was contemplating what to do.

Friend, how loved we are by God. How He wants our hearts to be aligned with His perfect will. And when we listen closely, heaven will whisper the will of God for our lives too. We might not get a visit from Gabriel, but we can experience a visit from the Spirit of God, who cares about our dashed dreams, our perfect little plans, and our disappointment that even with our best effort none of them are so perfect.

It Takes Courage to Believe God When Our Plans Are Interrupted

God cares about how we feel when our plans seem to go off the rails and He lovingly meets us in our deepest confusion to help us cope with our changed-up realities so that we can move forward, experience His greater purpose, and participate in the grander, broader picture He has in mind for us, His children.

How kind of God to reassure Joseph of Mary's faithfulness and God's plan for the baby;[4] how kind of God to buffer the blow of this change in their plans.

But, even so, Mary and Joseph were young and it must have taken a hefty amount of courage to process the changes coming their way. Had the wedding plans been made? The custom hand-calligraphed fig-leaf invitations sent out? We don't know. But we do know that Mary and Joseph were real people—like you and like me, with real desires, plans, and wedding dreams of their own. And we can imagine how disillusioning it must have been to wait—even longer—to consummate their marriage.

No matter how confusing the situation, Joseph didn't argue with the angel like Elizabeth's husband, Zechariah, had when Gabriel delivered the news of a baby for the older couple. Zechariah had asked Gabriel: "How can I be sure of this? I am an old man and my wife is well along in years."[5] Powerful Gabriel had no tolerance for his questioning God's authority, saying: "I stand in the presence of God, and I have been sent to speak to you and to tell you this good news. And now you will be silent and not able to speak until the day this happens, because you did not believe my words, which will come true at their appointed time."[6]

Friend, we can learn from Mary and Joseph to not bow to intimidation, fear, or questioning. I doubt Joseph wanted God to take his speech as Zechariah had experienced after questioning Gabriel. We'd be wise to learn from Joseph's unspoken surrender, which was like Mary's: "Let it be to me according to your word." A sharp contrast to Zechariah's "How can this be?"

Only God could birth courage and supernaturally position Mary and Joseph to parent the Savior of the world. And only Almighty God can supernaturally position women like you and me to leave behind our lives of fear and anxiety for confidence and freedom—especially when God's plan seems confusing.

God wants to use us whether we are young, like Mary, or along in years as Elizabeth. What will your response to God be when His brilliant light calls you to courageous living, friend?

The plan God has for each of us looks different than God's plan for Mary. But our willingness to faithfully surrender our lives to God's best plan is every bit as important. It takes courage to sell the house, go to the mission field, move an elderly parent into our home, become sole caregivers, downsize, become foster parents, have *another* baby, or come to grips with not being able to have a baby. It takes courage to be the bigger person when we've been wronged, to fight for right relationships, to faithfully listen for God's voice and follow His leading, to let go of our personal pride. Part of us wants to be surrendered like Mary, saying, "Let it be, Lord." But the educated, need-a-written-plan, got-to-fit-into-our-budget, need-to-have-security part of ourselves struggles to go with God's plan, asking, *How can this be?*

Mary's surrender left no room for a spirit of entitlement. But sometimes we want to tell God, *Don't sign me up unless I know for sure the ending will be a really good one. And by the way, God, instead of your plan for a donkey to carry me, I'll need to be escorted in a Rolls-Royce to Bethlehem. After all, I am the chosen woman of God, giving birth to Immanuel. Oh . . . and I'd like the finest room at the Ritz-Carlton Hotel, instead of that miserable manger! And could you keep those smelly animals away and the wise men also, because you know I'm a private person. . . . What? A feeding trough for my newborn's bed? I like my life tidy and clean, God. You understand my entitlement, right, Lord?*

Mary's beautiful surrender humbles me to the core. I wish I could say I've surrendered to everything God has ever positioned my life to be. But when unexpected death has happened, I've asked, "Why, God?" And when my husband's business went south several years ago, I wish I'd been courageous enough to say, "Let it be as you have spoken." Because on the other side of it, I see how God protected us, even in confusion and doubts. What a difference it would have made if we'd trusted even when we didn't understand.

Mary's response to Gabriel had nothing to do with her understanding everything she was facing. But it was a reflection of her trust in God. No matter what, she would obey and follow God's best leading. She had received God's word in her head, her heart, and also her womb. And in doing so she was able to give birth to the courage needed to bear her son, who would carry the world on His shoulders.

Mary's story inspires us to act courageously, even when our plans get flip-flopped, or when our lives seem confusing or unpredictable. When my brother's life was turned on its side, I asked him, "Why does it have to be you who gets cancer?" He courageously said, "Why not me? I'm no one special. The sun rises and sets on me like it does everyone else."

Only a person fully surrendered to God's higher authority can respond this way and mean it! I've witnessed it, time and time again: Jesus-loving friends and family members birthing courage, even when death was chasing them down, shoving their chemotherapy-balding heads down inside the trash can, throwing their guts up, yet able to confidently and courageously say, "God is good and I know He has a good plan for me!"

What about you? Do you believe God is good? That He has a good plan for you too?

Courage to Stay a Difficult Course

As Mary held the Redeemer of the world in her arms, she must have held closely the joy of knowing she and Joseph had courageously obeyed God's good plan for all of us. Her son's presence made her feel safe and protected. Do you think she was overwhelmed by her little bundle of agape love? Isn't every mother surprised to realize how love can run so deep, pierce one's heart the way motherhood does? What must it have felt like—holding perfect love in her arms?

Because time goes so quickly, Jesus' life must have reeled like a movie across the pages of Mary's life, quick clips of God's faithfulness consuming her: the "yes" to Gabriel; facing her family and Joseph; the marginal living her out-of-wedlock pregnancy caused; the fear for their journey to Bethlehem; fleeing from King Herod, who demanded all male children two years old and younger be killed; how the wise men King Herod had sent to spy had instead bowed down to worship her son—lavishing him with gifts and acknowledging his authority. God had protected her baby, her Savior, her King. Mary had been appointed by God to birth the Courage-Giver—and God had faithfully provided supernatural courage to stay the course, live out her assignments, stay true to God's plan, and keep believing with surrender.

Being a mother is hard work. It takes courage to accomplish the tasks required in raising our children: breakfast, get dressed, off to school, snacks at the end of the day, homework for hours on end, prepare dinner, bath time, pajama time, bed time. No matter how hard we try, we simply can't be it all or do it all. And it all goes so fast. . . .

My oldest son will be thirty-two years old this year, and I feel his life has been like a blip on a movie screen too. I relive the honor of holding him when his heart was breaking, lovingly mending bumps and scrapes on tiny knees, and watching him run, laugh, and play. It's hard to believe he is about the same age Jesus was when He was crucified.

When he comes for a visit, I find myself lingering, visually tracing the lines of his face. Wondering how his chubby cheeks turned into handsome, manly bone structure seemingly overnight. Clips of his elementary, junior high, high school, and college years seem to have run together in the ruckus of living. I wonder if Mary grieved, just a little, as Jesus grew up and became more and more independent of her? Or did she find comfort in becoming more and more dependent upon her son?

Knowing how much it hurt me when my son was mistreated at school or church, I can't imagine the pain Mary experienced when the crowd screamed, "*Crucify Him, Crucify Him!*" Imagine the panic at losing sight of her child, as the crowd pressed in around Him. Then catching a glimpse of His bleeding body, struggling beneath the weight of the cross. We mothers desperately want to protect our children. But it was out of Mary's hands. Everything Gabriel had said was set in motion. Jesus was no longer hers—Mary was His.

As His redeeming blood fell to the ground, did it saturate Mary's soul? This was her child's body—her *Savior's* body. Did the confusion clear in those painful moments? Only God could give a mother the kind of courage needed to bear such pain. Only God could keep her heart focused on the end result: the broken chains of death, God's people no longer sacrificing for forgiveness of sins. Her son *was* forgiveness, the spotless lamb to be slain. The cross provided Mary's soul and ours a path leading directly to God's heart: the way-maker, the truth-teller, the life-giver, providing grace for every sin.

Mary's story is a message of courage—equipping us for our great "terribles"—the confusing things that come our way, the things that rock our world, turn it on its axis, because the pain cuts so deep. This message gives us courage to say, "No matter what, I will trust you, Lord." So, grieve: your daughter's divorce, your best friend's betrayal, your pet parakeet's death, the loss of your job, the foreclosure of your home, the untimely surgery, the insurance deductible, your empty nest. But birth courage as you hope in your bright tomorrow and celebrate the joys of heaven ahead for those who believe. Imagine standing in the powerful presence of a holy God—Mary's son.

Courage to Live Your God-Story

Who would have guessed, a poor girl from Nazareth birthing the courageous Savior of the world? And who would have guessed, a little girl from Georgia with big fears and lots of insecurities writing a book about courage? How could I have known you would read this book and God would use His word to transform your thinking? Thank God now for the ruckus your obedient transformation is going to create. How the ripple effect of your faith and legacy will be felt and seen, for generations to come.

The story of Jesus didn't start at His birth, and it didn't end with His death. The most important part of your story and mine is not how we started this journey, but how we finish it. Let's finish strong, courageously displaying the hope of the gospel in the process of living. Show the world how God takes an average, fearful, stressed-out woman and births enough courage to not just skim by, but to overcome! He was, He is, and He will always be the Alpha and Omega, the beginning and the end—of each of our stories.

The story He is writing in your life will be way better than the one you have been working on.

Mary's son is here to help us in the process of living—making it possible for us to walk faithfully even when our child resists the truth of God's Word. You might feel like a big, fat failure of a mother. Don't believe that lie from hell. It's easy to believe the lie when you see no fruit, even though you did your best to raise your children in the faith: You took them to church, taught them God's Word, prayed by their bedside every night.

To you I say that He who began a good work in your child will be faithful to complete it.[7]

We can also find comfort in knowing that if we "train up a child in the way he should go; even when he is old he will not depart from it" (Proverbs 22:6).

I can't wait to sit with Mary in heaven, to find out how she courageously lived her life to completion without her son by her side. How she refocused her pain to the brand-new possibilities the gospel had provided her. I want to tell her what her son meant to me. How His coming changed my life, how her son helped me overcome big fears and insecurities. I want to thank her for all she went through to make freedom possible for me and for you too, friend. I think every day in heaven should be Mother's Day for Mary.

As we develop the courage of Mary to surrender our lives to God's higher authority, we will realize the awesome truth that our obstacles become opportunities to share the power of Jesus at work with the world. It's in unpredictable times that we find His supply endless. But sometimes in our darkest times we want to shake our fist in the air, angrily blaming God for taking away our brothers, sisters, mothers, fathers, children, friends, and pets. Once we surrender ourselves as God's property—trusting Him beyond the pain—then we can understand that God can't *take away* what He already owns.

To this day, I can hear the voices of my toddlers: *"It's mine, give it back!"* as they threw their pint-sized bodies on the floor, kicking and screaming. Explaining why they didn't have the right to take away toys that didn't belong to them was exhausting.

When God took my brother home to heaven, I threw my body across my bed. Weeping aloud, I asked Him, "Why? Why would You take him?" My brother's hand-scribbled note, written before passing—"*though he slay me, still I will praise him*"—seems similar to Mary's surrender to God's higher authority when she said, "Let it be to me according to your word." This kind of courage can't be fabricated, friend. This kind of courage is birthed when women like us turn our aching hearts toward God. I really don't think we've scratched the surface of understanding the power given us through Mary's son, Jesus. How His sacrifice became our freedom—helping us to be positive in the pain, hopeful in the loss, overcomers in life and in death.

It's okay to ask God why. Sometimes we ask wishing for different results, and sometimes we want to tell God what our end results should be. I think God wants us to walk out our life circumstances allowing Him to lead strong and sure.

My friend Sandy is a preschool teacher. One day a little boy announced to the class, "I'm in the charge!" Have you ever announced to God that you are in charge? Life is way more enjoyable when we let God be in charge. The little boy simply was not equipped to lead a classroom of children. That job was for a higher, wiser authority. Will you trust the higher, wiser authority with your life journey? Stop trying to control, fix, change, direct, or redirect your own life. The power of heaven is at work for you.

We are like the boy when we stand up to God, telling Him how our lives should go. Oh, friend, isn't it exhausting being in charge of God? Angel Gabriel sure seemed happy to be under the authority of God, proudly announcing whose presence he'd been standing in. Have you acknowledged God's authority? God knows what He's doing, friend. Let Him lead. If you insist on leading, you'll end up lost.

Perhaps today you woke up feeling a little less powerful, a lot more insignificant, and hugely unimportant. Take courage, friend. Cling to God's Word, which births courage for living. When life presses in hard around you, you'll be able to make lemonade and enjoy spending time in the powerful presence of God. In sweet times like this, I quiet myself and whisper,

"Jesus, come. Come near to my needy heart. Come and do the thing you came to do in me, through me, for the world and for your glory."

Do you think Mary will ask us, when we see her in heaven someday, if we birthed courage in our daily struggles? I think she'd love to hear our Jesus stories—how her son helped us courageously live this life. And I'd love to share with her how He helped me through some of the hardest experiences of my life. How I met Him while sitting in my little red chair in Mrs. Fountain's class, where I discovered the true colors of her son's love.

It was at the cross that Mary's true colors would shine brightest—a mother's faithfulness seen in the darkest hour of her life. Her child, the light of her world, would shine brighter than ever, crushing death and the grave for me and for you. Today marks a clean slate, giving us the opportunity to purify our hearts, step onto a new path with Almighty God in charge. Carry on, friend—go courageously!

COURAGE QUEST

1. Can you imagine an angel appearing to you? Imagine the angel telling you that you would conceive a child through the power of the Holy Spirit.
2. Why do you think God chose Mary and Joseph for this honored call?
3. Scripture reminds us that God has a purpose for our lives. What might God want to birth through you that could bring many to understand the fullness of His love? Do you need courage to accept the nudge of His spirit?
4. To think of Mary holding not only her son but her Savior in her arms does something to me. What about you? And

to think about her obedience to then loosen her grip, letting Jesus go to fulfill God's perfect plan of salvation for us, is about more than my heart can stand. How do these thoughts grip your heart?

5. Imagine the pain of watching your child die on a cruel Roman cross for the sake of others. Knowing all her son suffered through in order to bring us freedom, what might Mary say if she knew the many sins we struggle with today? How did Mary's story change your perspective or your need for courage?

9

Naked Courage

> Let him kiss me with the kisses of his mouth!
> For your love is better than wine;
> your anointing oils are fragrant;
> your name is oil poured out;
> therefore virgins love you.
>
> Song of Solomon 1:2–3

Do you hear the Shulammite woman's undeniable desire for her lover's kisses? His kisses are better than oil and wine, which were expensive commodities in ancient times; she was basically saying, "There is nothing more valuable than you." And makes it clear that a simple kiss wouldn't do!

The Shulammite woman wins a prize for straightforwardness:

> Draw me after you; let us run.
> The king has brought me into his chambers.
>
> Song of Solomon 1:4

Throughout the eight poetically written chapters of the Song of Solomon, the Shulammite woman and Solomon's love affair can be traced from the beginning of their first attractions to their courtship and marriage.

Both she and Solomon verbalize their individual yearnings with intricate details, exposing their loving affections by including taste, smell, touch, hearing, and sight. We'd have to be half dead *not* to be intrigued.

I realize some of us might find ourselves blushing a little as we read along. So before we keep going I pray we look deeper—at the broader, spiritual meanings each chapter paints—to see the unconditional, unrestrained, captivating love our Savior has for *us*. And how He longs for us to run to Him, escaping life's pressures and allowing His love to ease our worries, cares, and woes. He lovingly invites us to step away from the madding crowd, to separate ourselves from the noise and chaos of living, and experience the fullness of His unconditional love.

So, will you come along with me, friend? Going faithfully forward—touching on chapters 1 through 8 of the Song of Solomon to understand how freeing ourselves to be loved by the true lover of our souls also frees us to express love. May we heal, grow, and change through the challenges ahead. Come with me—without pretense, stripping away all the veneers—come naked and unafraid. Come with the kind of transparency that holds nothing back from the true lover of our souls—Jesus, the Son of God.

So . . . Lord, here we are. Women wanting to understand more of your heart through this very unique holy Word. We want more of you, Jesus. We want more wisdom, we want more courage to give, accept, and receive all the love you desire for us, your girls. Amen.

Courage to Be Quiet

At the start of chapter 1, the Shulammite woman's words exuded confidence, telling her love to *draw* her, or *lead* her into his chambers—his private places. Most women can understand needing or wanting precious "alone time" with the person we love most, right? In a noisy world, it's hard to escape from social media and other distractions. Alone time is important for healthy, loving relationships, but unfortunately, our alone time with God often is the thing most overlooked. What about you? Do you make time with God a priority? It takes courage to set healthy boundaries with our time, to make "quiet" a priority in the noisy world.

Such alone time was important to the Shulammite woman, and she made her needs very clear—she left little room for guessing what her true feelings and intentions were. From the outside looking in, it would seem she was a pretty confident woman, right? But do you think it's possible for a woman to act confident outwardly while struggling against terrible insecurities inwardly? I think the Shulammite woman would answer yes! One minute, she is expressing her love confidently; the next minute, her confidence is overshadowed by personal insecurities, as she tells Solomon:

> Do not gaze at me because I am dark,
> because the sun has looked upon me.
> My mother's sons were angry with me;
> they made me keeper of the vineyards,
> but my own vineyard I have not kept!
> Song of Solomon 1:6

Wow! Where did her confidence go? Where does our confidence go?

Have you ever put up a good front, acting like you had all the confidence in the world? Then, out of the blue, the voice of insecurity speaks for you? This happens to me too. And, sometimes, the voice of insecurity even prays for me! Yep, you read that right! Praying insecure prayers that go something like this:

> *Lord, I love you and I want you to draw me closer to your heart. Lead me through life. I know you love me, but don't you think someone else looks more like a speaker, a writer, a successful businesswoman, a teacher, a nurse—someone with thicker hair, whiter teeth, a thinner body? You see my dark spots, Lord, don't judge me, please. I know I should have taken better care of myself. I don't like the way I look and I don't like the way I feel; surely there's someone who could do better—someone who is the whole package, having beauty and brains?*

Friend, don't try to talk God out of passionately loving you. It's simply not possible. Do you try to talk God out of believing in you? Well, that won't work either! Like Solomon's unconditional expressions of love to the Shulammite woman, God loves you and me—just the way we are, with damaged skin and age spots, stretch marks and birthmarks. Our insecurities are a big deal to God and one of the reasons I wrote this book. Because if we are to experience the freedom of loving like the Shulammite woman and Solomon in our marriage relationships, then we must learn to love ourselves too.

Our deep insecurities and lack of confidence are every bit as important as the Shulammite woman's body-image issues. I feel confident in saying that God doesn't see us in our Ann Taylor or Anthropologie clothing. Instead, the Courage-Giver sees us completely naked and He loves every part of us—especially the places our low self-esteem has torn apart. As I said, the Song of Solomon is written metaphorically, to help us understand how the Savior would make a way for us to freely come into

His presence—His chambers—to experience the joy of being complete. Nothing stands between us and a holy God, friend. And He wants us to realize this love so we can confidently express love in broken areas of our lives.

Each time I catch a glimpse of my naked body in the mirror, I cringe a little. I don't know many women who like to gaze at their nakedness. As Solomon affirmed his love, some of us have a godly husband who tells us we are beautiful—but we don't believe him. And even if we did believe him, many of us wouldn't want to act out our feelings of love like the Shulammite woman, right? Perhaps you are perfectly happy writing cards and letters to express your love to your husband, or you'd rather cook his favorite meal. But sexual intimacies? No thank you, many would answer.

Some of us have been too deeply wounded by abusive men. Some have been emotionally neglected, or victims of sex trafficking or pornography. The list of reasons for not wanting to be sexually intimate is long, and super sad. I have tears in my eyes, wondering if your story matches any one of these. How I respect your ability to face each day, courageously fighting against fear and insecurity. How I pray you will find complete healing in the loving arms of your true love, Jesus, who has the power to transform your broken past into powerful tomorrows.

I want to be very careful here. I know many precious women reading this were sexually abused as children and still carry deep wounds today. Perhaps the thought of going into a man's private chamber to express physical love, as the Shulammite woman wanted to do, sickens you. I am so sorry, my sister. And I'd like to stop right here and pray for you.

Father, I ask you to take every thought captive by your holy power as my sister reads this chapter. Reveal your pure and holy love through the Shulammite woman's story.

Take her into your loving arms, healing from the inside out. Help her to experience the joy of love in its purest form, as you intended, in the days to come. Prove to her right here, right now, that YOU are the true lover of her soul who will never abuse or use her. Amen.

Dear friend, if reading this chapter causes you emotional pain because of your past experiences, you might want to skip to the next chapter. But before you do, know that the imagery and symbolism found here is intended to validate your worth. You are worth God giving himself up for. He is the bridegroom who will never objectify or abuse you. His is not a physical love but a Father's love seeking to protect you from harm, treasure every part of you, honor you at the highest level, and redeem the painful past with His powerful love. His love is a heart-and-soul, eternal kind of love—the purest love possible—with the power to heal you completely.

If you *want* to keep reading, here's what I'd like you to do: Take a break and make a cup of your favorite tea or coffee, then snuggle under a favorite comfy blanket. Finish reading the rest of Song of Solomon, chapters 1 through 8. (Please don't stop reading until all eight chapters are completed.) And if you don't own a Bible, or you don't have it with you, no worries—simply read online, using your favorite version of the Bible on your cell phone or tablet.

Courage to Respect Ourselves

There's so much controversy surrounding sexuality today. This book is about courage and I think it takes courage to ask God what is the right way to express and receive love. As I type this, I hear Johnny Lee, a country music singer from the 1980s, singing his number-one hit song, "Lookin' for Love" (in all the wrong places). Johnny Lee sings about how he spent a lifetime looking for love in bars, seeking good-time lovers. He was trying to find his ideal love, hoping to spot it by the look in her eyes. He wanted more than a friend. He wanted a lover and turned to strangers because he was so desperate to find a true love.[1]

Our insecurities sometimes cause us to see ourselves as deficient. And our insecurities choose the kind of love we *think we deserve.* The Shulammite woman inspires us to pursue love carefully and wisely. Friend, don't settle for second best. Wait for the one your soul will truly love. Please wait!

I'm so blessed to hang out with lots of people in their twenties and thirties. They openly share their very real struggles to remain sexually pure. Some share stories of their one-night stands, their life-altering "big mistakes" ending with pregnancies and sexually transmitted diseases. It breaks my heart to hear their inner longings for love—and how they gave themselves away to someone who didn't deserve the gift of their beautiful, treasured bodies.

> On my bed by night
> I sought him whom my soul loves;
>   I sought him, but found him not.
> I will rise now and go about the city,
>   in the streets and in the squares;
> I will seek him whom my soul loves.
>   I sought him, but found him not.
> The watchmen found me
>   as they went about in the city.
> "Have you seen him whom my soul loves?"
> Scarcely had I passed them
>   when I found him whom my soul loves.
> I held him, and would not let him go
>   until I had brought him into my mother's house,
>   and into the chamber of her who conceived me.

> I adjure you, O daughters of Jerusalem,
> by the gazelles or the does of the field,
> that you not stir up or awaken love
> until it pleases.
>
> Song of Solomon 3:1–5

If you had the misperception that God is a fuddy-duddy who thinks sex is bad, then the Shulammite woman should clear up your confusion. God is a loving Father who wants His children to experience true love, in the right context, and in the right order. His love is not a sexual love, but the purest, highest level of love available to us. He sees us, His bride, as flawlessly beautiful. Others might see the fat girl, the skinny girl, an old girl, the acne face, but God sees His beloved beauty, the one He chose from the beginning of time.

The concept of "naked courage" helps us stop hiding any part of ourselves from Him.

So Lord, we come—without covering our insecurities or our shame. We stand naked before you, bringing the woman we so desperately wish we were not, choosing to be transformed into the woman you see we can be. We thank you for how the Song of Solomon reminds us of your gentle, loving whispers to our needy souls. Thank you for the way your love validates us: "You are altogether beautiful, my love; there is no flaw in you" (Song of Solomon 4:7).

Thank you, Lord, that although we are flawed by a sinful, fallen world, you see no flaws in us, because you are the true lover of our soul and we hide our flawed selves in you. In a Photoshopped world of perfection, where airbrushed images are our benchmark for true beauty, we thank you. We know you want us to find and experience true love.

Courage Helps Us Discern True Love

> Enjoy life with the wife whom you love, all the days of your vain life that he has given you under the sun.
>
> Ecclesiastes 9:9

This is what God wanted from the beginning. And before the sinful fall of man, there was paradise.[2]

Imagine—

Crystal-clear water falling from high places, spilling into shimmering, blue reservoirs—so transparent one can see right to the bottom where every aquatic creature scurries about.

Lush green foliage envelopes the magnificent Garden of Eden, as far as the eye can see, in electric shades of yellow, purple, orange, and red. Tall, majestic trees create breathtaking canopies proudly dancing in the breeze, providing the perfect comforting shade.

Peaceful order surrounds you, and birds sing joyfully—celebrating their perfect paradise home—and so do you.

Radiant beams of sunlight caress your naked body. Balmy breezes make your skin feel alive with a sense of wonder as you inhale and exhale contentedly, pure oxygen filling your lungs with each cleansing breath.

You see him from a distance, the man you were created as a helpmate for. He is perfectly formed in every way. As his eyes meet yours, he slowly begins to linger over every line, every trace, of your delicately created physique. He is enthralled by your beauty—mesmerized by your perfection. *You* are his only desire. There is no other creature that compares to you.

Imagine, all of creation is bathed in innocence—unbroken. No sin. No shame. No regret. As you stand before your lover—Adam—your confidence soars to new heights, knowing: You are his missing piece.

That was God's plan, before the fall of man.

Once Eve ate the forbidden fruit, her eyes were opened and she realized her nakedness that had been sacred, pure, holy. And she was ashamed. God told her she would long for her husband's affection, and so do we.[3] Unless Jesus is the lover of our soul, I'm afraid we will keep looking for love in all the wrong places.

Our ultimate fulfillment always leads back to Jesus. But coming to Him requires naked courage, bringing the shame of Eve along with all that you are, placing your whole identity *inside* of all that He is. Once you do, no other lover will satisfy your soul. Will you allow God to unveil your beauty, friend?

It takes courage to recognize the beauty we bring to the world, and even more courage to step out and actually *bring it*. It's hard to strip off our old ways of thinking, our old patterns of living and come to God with naked courage, seeking His face honestly, so we can be transformed inwardly. The overflow of this inward transformation will affect every choice going forward.

A young single girl told me once that she'd lost her virginity and liked it. I said, "Guess what? You liked it because God designed it, and what God designs is *good*. But outside of marriage, sex is very destructive. Look to the Shulammite woman's example and don't open your heart or your door to someone who will rob you blind and leave you, *and your baby,* crying." It takes courage to respect God's principles, but you can be sure a loving God always sets His standards based on His great love for you. Will you ask God for courage to respect yourself?

> Our sister is young;
> she has no breasts.
> What will we do for our sister
> on the day she is spoken for?
> If she is a wall,
> we will build a silver parapet on it.

If she is a door,
we will enclose it with cedar planks.
Song of Solomon 8:8–9 HCSB

If you've ever experienced criticism from family members about your body, you'll have lots of compassion for the Shulammite woman. But what I love here is that no matter what her family thought about her physical appearance, she was able to love and embrace the woman God created her to be and she was excited about receiving the nonjudgmental love of Solomon.

Then in verse 10, the Shulammite woman speaks for herself, now with confidence, and she has found peace with her physical appearance. Oh, if we could do the same, dear friends:

I am a wall
and my breasts like towers.
So in his eyes I have become
like one who finds peace.

I think this was her way of saying: "My breasts might look small, but they are 'out-of-reach towers' to anyone undeserving of my affections." Although her desires were very real, she would not lower her standards and was able to experience peace: "In his eyes I have become like one who finds peace." There is peace in *not* looking to others to affirm that we are enough. Who do you look to, friend?

God wants us to make peace with our bodies. Have you made peace with yours? It's part of the inner healing and it's a key element in leaving behind our fear and insecurity for a life of confidence and freedom. Will you come to Jesus, the lover of your soul, and find peace in knowing His is the standard to follow? Come with your double-D or double-A cups, and don't try to be something you aren't. Your friend has a sexier way about her? So what! Your goal is to have a *godly* way about you!

You can be godly and desirable, and sexy *inside* the chambers of love. You don't have to conform to the ways of the world, but it takes courage not to. You don't have to wear a dress that barely covers your bum, or expose your breasts over the top of your blouse to get God's attention. He loves you "as is." With age spots and graying hair, with saggy breasts and the jelly belly hidden away inside your Spanx.

If you feel like your past is too full of sin and insecurities, you are the very reason Jesus came. He was stripped down at the cross to give us naked courage, making it possible for us to strip off our old selves to be clothed in His righteousness.

Five Courageous Steps to Take

There are five important things the Shulammite woman did to enhance her relationship with Solomon: She showed interest, pursued, complimented, nurtured, and gave a wise warning to beware of "little foxes."

1. **Show interest:** Can you imagine the response you'd get if you told your husband, "Everything about you interests me. Whatever is important to you is important to me, my love."

   The Shulammite woman showed her lover interest by asking Solomon to tell her about what his soul loves, and by inquiring about his activities:

   > Tell me, you whom my soul loves,
   > where you pasture your flock,
   > where you make it lie down at noon.
   > Song of Solomon 1:7

   Would your man fall over with a heart attack if you met him with, "My lover, tell me all about your day. I want to hear every word you have to say, because my soul loves you!"?

True confession: Sometimes, when hubby comes home I am either on the phone or social media. Although ashamed, I *am* writing a chapter entitled "Naked Courage," so I must come transparently too! What about you? Have you ever been guilty of only half listening to your husband as he debriefs about his day? Every few words, you *might* interject an insincere "hummmm" or "Oh my!"

2. **Pursue:** In bed at night, the Shulammite woman "sought him whom my soul loves."[4] She held him "and would not let him go."[5]

   When was the last time you initiated sex with your husband? Please know that I'd never suggest sex will fix your problems. But as we've learned in Song of Solomon, everyone is worth pursuing, and in a healthy, loving marriage to pursue your husband is a powerful way of expressing how much he is loved and valued, not only by you, but by God. Remember, you are the only naked woman in the room. There's no one like you!

3. **Compliment:** The Shulammite woman tells her lover he is "beautiful, my beloved, truly delightful."[6]

   While my husband wouldn't want me to tell him he's beautiful, I'm learning a few tips from the Shulammite woman about expressing my appreciation for how hard he works to provide for our family, how nice he looks, and how blessed I am that he's *all* mine.

   A woman at a conference bragged about her husband to me, and I asked, "Have you told him?" She said, "You know, I need to!" "Yes, text him today," I said, "and tell him the nice things you said to me about him."

On a humorous note, I must be honest and say I wouldn't find it romantic at all if my husband texted or whispered, "Your hair is like a flock of goats" or "Your teeth are like a flock of shorn ewes that have come up from the washing, all of which bear twins, and not one among them has lost its young" (Song of Solomon 4:1–2).

I guess the fact that he noticed that I've not lost any teeth should be a compliment! But I might be moved to action if he said, "My beloved speaks and says to me: 'Arise, my love, my beautiful one, and come away'" (Song of Solomon 2:10).

Friend, who needs *Fifty Shades of Grey* with this kind of reading at our fingertips, and straight from God's holy Word?

4. **Nurture:** The Shulammite woman nurtured her relationship, as in verse 2:10 above. Think of ways to help your husband escape or "come away" from the stresses of life. The most attractive part of the Song of Solomon, to me, is the mutual affection expressed. Remember, it takes two people working together to create a healthy relationship.

5. **Catch the Little Foxes:** Another wise warning from our Shulammite friend is to:

> "Catch the foxes for us, the little foxes that spoil the vineyards, for our vineyards are in bloom."
>
> Song of Solomon 2:15

If your relationship is in full bloom—growing and thriving—then please guard it with all your might. Beware of the little foxes creeping in to destroy. And if your marriage is in trouble read on to see two little foxes that seem harmless, but can kill the blooms in your intimacy.

Beware of Little Foxes—for Wives:

1. **Be a lover, not a mother:** Your husband wants you to be his lover, not his mother. He had a mother. And you are not her.

2. **Don't nag:** Nagging is neither attractive nor helpful in striving for passion, love, and intimacy in marriage. What you'll get is a shut-down, closed-off man. I'm not suggesting your needs aren't important, but I am urging that you carefully pick your timing and consider how you express your needs.

> Better to live on a corner of the roof
> than share a house with a quarrelsome wife.
> Proverbs 21:9 NIV

> Better to live in the desert
> than with a quarrelsome and nagging wife.
> Proverbs 21:19 NIV

Beware of Little Foxes—for Singles:

1. **Guard your heart:** The Shulammite woman wisely says: "Don't arouse love or awaken love until it so desires" (Song of Solomon 3:5 NIV).

2. **Take your time and choose wisely your love:** "All night long I looked for the one my heart loves" (Song of Solomon 3:1 NIV).

I think the Shulammite woman is wisely warning us to not settle for the first person who gives us attention, but to wait for true and lasting love.

A dear friend of mine was almost forty years old before she got married. She had dreamed of a man who would love her unconditionally since she was a teenager. Many times she wondered why God refused to answer her prayers. Now she realizes that what appeared to be God's withholding was actually His protection over her. Recently, she shared that she feels she should never have gotten married. She looked for love in a man rather than God's perfect love, and she had settled for the first man who seemed to be the real deal. Although the two have worked hard to keep their vows and honor each other, the road hasn't been an easy one.

So, I have to ask all the single ladies reading this book if you will be satisfied waiting and looking for your true love or will you rush in and live a miserable life, paying the price for giving in to an impatient need for a lover? And what if your love *never* comes along? Will you be content in your singleness?

I met a young woman at a writers conference recently. As she expressed her desire to write a book, I didn't expect to hear what she shared:

> I'm single and content in my singleness, and want to write a book to help other singles celebrate their time of singleness. If I never get married, I will be okay! Jesus completes me. He is my husband. I know my Bridegroom is coming for me, someday soon, and I don't feel a void.
>
> Unnamed Friend

Friend, I hope our time spent in the Song of Solomon has given you naked courage to not shrink back from God. To allow Him to be your true love. As you bare your whole self before God, I pray you will find true and lasting freedom to enjoy your life inside of His love. Listen carefully to the voice of your True Love singing over you. Feel the gravity of His holy Word drawing you to the absolute truth of His heart. He will never compound your insecurities or your fears. He will heal you. Will you *let* Him heal you? You are His beautiful bride and there is no one like you. Will you prepare for the Bridegroom to come?

Come, holding nothing back—courageously naked and unashamed.

COURAGE QUEST

1. What did you learn from the Shulammite woman?
2. Did you find any little foxes in your relationship?
3. Have you ever thought of Christ as the true lover of your soul? When a person fails to express love, do you know without a shadow of a doubt there is a God who thinks you are beautiful in every way?
4. What inspired you most as you read about the Shulammite woman's love for Solomon?
5. Did you learn better ways of giving and receiving love?

10

Crocodile Faith

As Jochebed held her son Moses in her arms, fear and anxiety must have consumed her. She could never have dreamt she would be in this position: forced to hide her baby boy among the papyrus reeds of the Nile River banks. It was unthinkable. In ancient Egypt, the Nile River was the source of life, providing water to local farms, fields, and families—central to survival for ancient Egypt. But the Nile was also infested with crocodiles, some as long as twenty feet—ambushers who waited patiently along the river's edge until the opportune time when they would crush their helpless prey between their massive jaws.[1] And prey didn't get more helpless than Jochebed's three-month-old baby boy.

Or was her son Moses *truly* helpless?

A little backstory will help to set the stage for what brought Jochebed to the river's edge that fateful day.

There was a new king in town—I mean Egypt. And from his perspective, the Israelites had become way too numerous for his liking. Fear fed his paranoia, creating a monster and convincing the king that if the Israelite nation continued to multiply, they would eventually overtake his kingdom. As Pharaoh's insecurities grew, so did his desperate need to control the population of God's chosen people.

> But the people of Israel were fruitful and increased greatly; they multiplied and grew exceedingly strong, so that the land was filled with them. Now there arose a new king over Egypt, who did not know Joseph. And he said to his people, "Behold, the people of Israel are too many and too mighty for us. Come, let us deal shrewdly with them, lest they multiply, and, if war breaks out, they join our enemies and fight against us and escape from the land." Therefore, they set taskmasters over them to afflict them with heavy burdens. They built for Pharaoh store cities, Pithom and Raamses. But the more they were oppressed, the more they multiplied, and the more they spread abroad. And the Egyptians were in dread of the people of Israel. So they ruthlessly made the people of Israel work as slaves and made their lives bitter with hard service, in mortar and brick, and in all kinds of work in the field. In all their work they ruthlessly made them work as slaves.
>
> Exodus 1:7–14

How could *slaves* pose such a threat to a powerful king? There was an undeniable power resting on the Israelite community of God's chosen people, and this power irritated the daylights out of the king. His concerns were for *his* position, *his* authority, *his* power—his own fears had shaken him to the core of his identity. Leaving us wondering, who was truly the slave?

Evil Pharaoh, oh, the depths he would go to in order to control his kingdom.

> Then the king of Egypt said to the Hebrew midwives, one of whom was named Shiphrah and the other Puah, "When you

> serve as midwife to the Hebrew women and see them on the birthstool, if it is a son, you shall kill him, but if it is a daughter, she shall live." But the midwives feared God and did not do as the king of Egypt commanded them, but let the male children live. So the king of Egypt called the midwives and said to them, "Why have you done this, and let the male children live?" The midwives said to Pharaoh, "Because the Hebrew women are not like the Egyptian women, for they are vigorous and give birth before the midwife comes to them."
>
> Exodus 1:15–19

Courage to Worship God Above All Others

Can you imagine Pharaoh's shock and dismay when he received news of the midwives' refusal to execute his evil schemes? They might as well have smashed an entire humble pie in Pharaoh's prideful face. And to hear they feared their God more than their king? What an offense! No one feared God more than they feared Pharaoh. Well, no one who mattered anyway. But these women mattered to God. And more importantly, God mattered to them. Whether stubbornness or courage, no one knows, but they refused to compromise themselves for the sake of wickedness as the king had demanded. What about you, friend? Do you compromise right for wrong or do you honor God in every way?

Pharaoh's oversized pride must have suffered even more as he listened to the midwives clucking on about the strength of the Hebrew women—how no midwife assistance was needed and how they completed the birthing process before the midwives even arrived on the birthing scene. Their comments were crafty and comparative, suggesting the Egyptian women were weaker, less capable. This added fuel to Pharaoh's already blazing insecurities.

God's undeniable hand of protection was on the midwives, and on the Hebrew communities of Egypt—otherwise the king would have ended the midwives' lives right then and there.

Friend, God never overlooks integrity. And although the focus of this chapter is on Jochebed, we cannot overlook the other courageous women who powerfully and prophetically took part in the whole of her amazing story. And we cannot overlook the importance of fearfully serving our King of heaven, instead of the Pharaohs in our lives. Their acts of faith, courage, and integrity brought about blessings. As they held fast to their convictions, obeying the heart of God instead of participating in evil, their powerful God blessed them with so much more.

> So God dealt well with the midwives. And the people multiplied and grew very strong. And because the midwives feared God, he gave them families.
>
> Exodus 1:20–21

A promise had been made years before this story rolled out, when God told Abraham that he would bless him and multiply his offspring:

> "I will surely bless you, and I will surely multiply your offspring as the stars of heaven and as the sand that is on the seashore. And your offspring shall possess the gate of his enemies, and in your offspring shall all the nations of the earth be blessed, because you have obeyed my voice."
>
> Genesis 22:17–18

Well . . . Pharaoh wasn't about to give up so easily. He devised a plan B: Cast every male Hebrew child into the Nile. Problem solved! A Hebrew girl can't produce more Hebrew children without a male to mate with, right? Right! Ol' Pharaoh thought he'd solved his problem completely, this time.

> Then Pharaoh commanded all his people, "Every son that is born to the Hebrews you shall cast into the Nile, but you shall let every daughter live."
>
> Exodus 1:22

Courageous Jochebed comes on the scene, in Exodus chapter 2. Having married a man from the house of Levi, Jochebed conceived a child quickly after the vows were spoken. She gave birth to a *boy* child! Can you imagine the fear that replaced Jochebed's joy? Oh, the dreams she must have had for her son—the wild aspirations a newborn inspires. But Jochebed was faced with a reality that most of us have never had to face: the genocide of every Hebrew male baby in Egypt.

No birth announcements were sent out, no signs placed outside their tent proclaiming, "Look what the stork brought! It's a boy!" Quietly, she and her hubby managed to hide their child for three months:

> When she could hide him no longer, she took for him a basket made of bulrushes and daubed it with bitumen and pitch. She put the child in it and placed it among the reeds by the river bank. And his sister stood at a distance to know what would be done to him.
>
> Exodus 2:3–4

Pharaoh was oblivious to the courage at work in the heart of a Hebrew mother named Jochebed. She was crafty, faithful, and determined, and she resigned herself that whatever came her way, evil would not destroy her child. I've jokingly said there's a momma bear inside every mother's heart—don't mess with her babies, or you'll get a little taste of her "momma-bear wrath." You momma bears reading this can relate, right? I thought so. . . . Growl!

Oh, the weeping. Not just a day, or two, or a week—but for months. I can almost hear it in my mind, feel the weight of sadness, reach out and touch the gut-wrenching despair of the Hebrew mothers along the water's edge. Having birthed two sons of my own, knowing the depth of love I feel for them. I can't begin to imagine the depth of suffering the women experienced, the level of courage needed to breathe the next breath, live another day, do a normal task after their sons were ripped from their loving arms, thrown into a river, shredded into tiny little pieces by blood-thirsty crocodiles. Can you?

Perhaps you *can* imagine. You lost custody of your child? Your lawyer had told you it could never happen. Had the abortion? Gave your child up for adoption? Lost a child to a tragic car accident? Someone's lies ripped your child from your life, and left your child believing an evil lie. Your arms and your life feel empty.

Jochebed would cry with you. She'd have compassion. Slowly lowering her basket down into the murky waters of the Nile meant she'd draw back empty hands. She'd run out of solutions. No other plan made sense. Pharaoh had commanded that every Hebrew male baby be thrown into the Nile, and she'd obeyed half of his command, at least. Her child was in the Nile but there was covering and protection around him, and it wasn't the basket made of bitumen and pitch; it was the covering of God's spirit.

His spirit must have hovered over Jochebed too, comforting her mother's heart as she let go. And God will do the same for me and you, friend. I'm so glad it's possible to *choose to act courageously* when we are fresh out of courage. As Jochebed *chose courage*, she was no longer a slave to fear. Sometimes we allow the thing we fear most to paralyze us, to stop us dead in our tracks, hinder our futures, breach our joy, and stump our spiritual growth.

And so, Lord, we come. Courageously. Asking you to set us free from all unhealthy self-images. From the words of others that have paralyzed us so. From the deepest wounds of our past that have held us back. When life breaks, we courageously cling to you, Father, and we choose to courageously "let go" so you can fulfill your better plan for our lives, for the lives of our children, our loved ones. Our babies and grandbabies yet unborn. For every future generation connected to our bloodline. May we not hold on too tightly, or love anything more than you, so that we can experience true freedom, as you intended on the cross. Amen.

Choosing Courage Means Choosing Faith

We usually can't see the answers to know where our painful roads will end. And it's by faith that we can choose crocodile courage: knees bent down by the river's edge in what feels like the most dangerously painful territories we've ever known. There are no easy answers for life's big problems: the evils of this world, the deaths, divorces, foreclosures, abuses, and neglects. But I believe surrender is a beautiful way we can consecrate our lives to God. And as we consecrate ourselves—holding nothing back—we faithfully release the power of God into our futures:

> Now the daughter of Pharaoh came down to bathe at the river, while her young women walked beside the river. She saw the basket among the reeds and sent her servant woman, and she took it. When she opened it, she saw the child, and behold the baby was crying. *She took pity on him and said, "This is one of the Hebrews' children."*
>
> Exodus 2:5, emphasis added

It must have been difficult for Jochebed to pry her loving fingers free from the basket holding her precious cargo. What is God asking you to pry your loving hands away from? Your husband, a wayward child, a grandchild? Your health? Your finances? There's no way Jochebed could have perceived that her courageous act of letting go would in actuality loose heaven's power, demanding the enemy become her source of provision. Jochebed gave up her rights as mother, but still was able to maintain her intimacy with her son.

> Then his sister said to Pharaoh's daughter, "Shall I go and call you a nurse from the Hebrew women to nurse the child for you?" And Pharaoh's daughter said to her, "Go." So the girl went and called the child's mother. And Pharaoh's daughter said to her, "Take this child away and nurse him for me, and I will give you your wages." So the woman took the child and nursed him. When the child grew older, she brought him to Pharaoh's daughter, and he became her son. She named him Moses, "Because," she said, "I drew him out of the water."
>
> Exodus 2:7–10

Jochebed's faithfulness would take her child from slave to the palace as an adopted child of the king. We, too, are heirs to a throne and have been adopted as children of the most-high God. Jochebed didn't scream out to Pharaoh's daughter, "He's my son!" Instead, she humbled herself, positioning Moses higher so God's ultimate glory could be revealed through him.

Friend, be encouraged. God sees your past, and your current fears, and He has already put into place a plan that will ensure your future freedom:

> So if the Son sets you free, you will be free indeed.
>
> John 8:36

Can you imagine the joy Jochebed must have felt? God had set His supernatural plan into motion. She would not have to walk away from her son, not just yet. Instead, the king's daughter would *pay* her to nurse her beloved baby.

Friend, when you and I walk humbly and submit to God's higher authority in our lives, He faithfully lifts the thing we thought we'd lost forever from the miry clay and sets us on a new path, with a new plan, to enable us to experience the best days ever!

What joy! Jochebed's son would not be eaten by crocodiles. Instead, he would be brought into the house of Pharaoh, treated as an honored son, provided abundantly for, educated in Egyptian culture, and prepared for the day when he would fulfil his purpose—setting God's people free.

And to think all of this could have been avoided if Pharaoh had respected the history of Jochebed's people. His cold heart had no regard for the years of legacy left by the fine sons of Israel.

> Now there arose a new king over Egypt, who did not know Joseph.
>
> Exodus 1:8

There's a reason why God noted that the king didn't remember Joseph. It's a warning to us all not to forget God, and to keep the examples of other godly people close to our heart so we can model our lives on their courage and faithfulness. But this new Pharaoh was so self-driven, the only history he was concerned with was the history *he* was making.

How could Jochebed expect better from the new king? After all, a heart far removed from God is a heart left to its own demise, right? May our hearts never be left so, friend. I'm so glad to know you have a heart to grow in God's Word so that your life can be marked by courageous living, like the women noted throughout the pages of this book. It's so pleasing to God that we study, remember, and apply the wisdom of faithful souls who lived before us.

The Hebrew people respected the great sons of Israel; so we can imagine how Pharaoh's disrespect would have been a hard pill for the Israelite community to swallow. Some of us with edgier attitudes would have gladly given the new Pharaoh a little history lesson! I'm sure we'd *try* to keep it as godly as possible, of course! Gently but firmly reminding him that on the chronological list were far more than just names, they were some of the most highly respected, courageous, godly men of old—willing to risk everything for their powerful, faithful God, and having more courage and leadership in their pinkies than Pharaoh had in both hands together. How dare he disregard these men and women of valor? How dare we?

If only Pharaoh had shown respect for Jochebed's ancestors, a generation of male descendants could have been spared death in the Nile. If he'd remembered Joseph, surely he would have been impressed that even after being thrown into a pit by his jealous brothers, he was brought into a previous Pharaoh's palace a slave but became second in command over Egypt.[2]

Courage to Honor the Past While Moving Into Our Future

By now you might be thinking, "Okay, LaTan! But what does this have to do with my becoming a courageous woman of God?" It has everything to do with it, friend. Trust me, respecting the past and those who paved the way to ensure safety for our sons and daughters helps us remember what we stand to lose. I hope we will teach our children to celebrate the blessing of our freedoms today and guard our future liberty carefully.

To not show respect for Joseph meant overlooking the courage of those who'd made Egypt what it was. To not show respect to past and present leaders of our great nation is showing the same kind of disregard for authority. And without getting on my political soapbox, I have to add that God wants us to respect our leaders—whether we agree with their policies or not.

Jochebed's physical actions surrendered to her authority, Pharaoh, as evil as he was. But her heart surrendered to the higher authority of God, when she courageously placed her son in the Nile River that day. She let go of a mother's dream for her child. Every plan she and her husband had made they tucked away into the reeds by the riverbank. I'm convinced that when a woman's heart is in line with the heart of God's will, God's plans *become* her own plans. It's easy to let go of our own agenda when we crave God's agenda more.

So you wanted your child to be a doctor, and he wants to be in a band. Put your disappointment into your custom-made basket, and place your child into the Nile, friend. As scary as it is, a surrendered life is a powerful life. Surrendering reshapes our future and our children's futures, and has the power to reshape the destiny of an entire nation of God's faithful people.

Poor Jochebed found herself facing the crocodiles because of an angry Pharaoh who'd let fear and intimidation consume him. How I want to put on my rose-colored glasses, to believe the king could muster interest in the notable ancestry of his slaves. But centuries of colorful, artistic memories etched into the palace walls wouldn't change his nasty disrespect. In his mind, those days were long gone. A new day had dawned, and Pharaoh was the man in charge.

But God never forgets our faithfulness or our ability to be courageous in the face of conflict, fear, or impending danger. I believe that, no matter what the news says, no matter the number of circling crocs in our rivers, good days are ahead for us—for our children, and our children's children. We can find comfort knowing that if God thought it important for us to remember Joseph then He has also remembered us. Not one single detail in the history of our lives has God overlooked. Pharaoh might have pushed the past faithfulness of God's people aside to pursue his own selfish ambitions, but God hadn't forgotten.

It was from a small Hebrew family that an impressive nation had grown. God had noted every struggle and every success: Joseph's ability to interpret dreams, his faithful rise to power as manager of Egypt's resources, the grace he extended to the brothers who had betrayed him, bringing them into the palace, how he'd wisely bought back the land of Egypt for the king, and provided seeds for the people to harvest when they would otherwise have starved to death.[3] These memories would only have fueled Pharaoh's mounting fears. The power of God was plain to see.

I think Pharaoh saw freedom in their eyes, though their bodies were in chains. If the king was to control them, he had to contain them. Friend, did you know that's also the goal of your enemy, Satan: to control and contain you? Put your whole, entire, worn-out self inside of God's protective care. Don't wait until things make sense, do it especially when things *don't* make sense. And when God finally draws you from your crocodile-infested waters, it will be through a source you never saw coming. Never forget how your faithful God did it for a Hebrew woman named Jochebed. Never forget, He can do it in the life of a woman like you!

God's appointed baby, Moses—the one who had an anointing on his life, the one who would be spared a crocodile's death because of one momma's courageous spirit—would become a deliverer.

God had blessed this courageous woman of the Bible, Jochebed, by sparing her offspring, Moses. Two midwives, concerned more with courageously following after God than schmoozing into the good graces of a paranoid, evil king, were to thank for Moses' life being spared. Their brave decision—to go against Pharaoh's wishes and follow God's—is not to be overlooked. These women were every bit as courageous, and every bit as powerful, as the sons of Israel. They remained true to God, no matter how dangerous or risky that was. But isn't it better to live on the edge with God than to give in to pressure?

Courage Frees Our Soul

Jochebed might have been enslaved by man, but her soul was free. And the waters of the Nile might have appeared scary and dangerous, but from God's perspective those dangerous waters were heaven at work. Sometimes things don't appear the way they truly are.

This reminds me of a television cartoon series, *Courage the Cowardly Dog*, that made its debut in 1999. It follows Courage, an easily frightened lavender dog. He was abandoned as a puppy after his parents were forcibly sent into outer space by a crazed veterinarian. He lives in an attached garage near the fictional town of Nowhere, Kansas, with Muriel Bagge, a sweet-natured Scottish woman, and her American husband, Eustace Bagge, a grouchy, selfish, greedy man who constantly harasses Courage. Courage was found in an alley by Muriel, who took him home as her own. Courage is controlled by fear, and his mind plays tricks on him, making him think that he's in real danger when he's not, or that there are monsters about to jump out or grab him. But it's all his imagination.[4]

Friend, Satan cannot control a soul that has been truly set free by God, and he hates it. And as much as Pharaoh hated his inability to control the growing Israelite nation, he could not. Like Courage the Cowardly Dog, the king's imagination got the best of him.

Jochebed and the midwives courageously dealt with the realities given them: the authority of an evil king but overriding respect for the authority of an all-powerful God. And their brave choices produced crocodile faith that would keep God's pint-sized leader, Moses, out of harm's way, preserving him for his very important future purposed positioning.

Did Jochebed feel cursed? Like us, she must have fought against a few tormenting questions in her momma-head: *What loving mother would leave her baby in danger to keep him from danger?* No matter how Jochebed reasoned, it made no sense to leave precious baby Moses at the mercy of the Nile, and yet somehow, it made all the sense in the world.

Mothers break under the pressure of the cries of their children. We'll go night after night without sleep, work our fingers to the bone, sacrifice our last dollar for our children. Making our children's lives as peaceful as possible is often more of a concern than making their lives as godly as possible. Jochebed's circumstances demanded that she look to God for strength. How else could she understand her overwhelming life circumstances? How can we?

Do you need a little of Jochebed's crocodile faith today, friend? The kind of faith that puts everything as we've known it at risk, realizing God has a better plan than we can possibly imagine. This is a whole new level of courage to live out. As we courageously surrender our lives to God's keeping we can also release fear.

Some of us feel challenged by Jochebed's courage to surrender the dream of conceiving a child of our own. The years of weeping into our pillow at night have taken their toll. We don't understand why we have to be enslaved to a body that won't produce, when every day others are aborting little ones.

Friend, I pray for God to help you. Will you lay the pain down at His capable feet with Jochebed's crocodile faith? I pray we will trust Him, even when we cannot see with our own eyes God's amazing future plans for us.

Courage to Release What We Hold Most Dear

Jochebed's release of her precious son Moses, as dangerous and as gut-wrenching as it might have been, ultimately ushered in freedom for an entire nation of God's people. Her story is an important resource that shows us how putting our faith into action sometimes requires greater courage than we can imagine. Will you courageously release to God everything you hold most dear: husband, children, job, and friendships? Releasing these to God can make us feel afraid and vulnerable, but when we do we receive God's protective covering and blessing. Jochebed gave her child over to God's best leading, and in her letting go many were transformed and freed.

What are you afraid of? When the strength of God is seen in us, the enemy loses his grip, friend. Our best plans for our children are no match for the plans God has for them.

Perhaps your single goal as a mother is to make sure your child experiences a perfect life. Letting go of the control might mean moving out of your home and that would be as scary as placing baby Moses into the crocodile-infested Nile waters. It's one thing to care for and diligently love our children, and another thing to cling. When we hold on and desperately try to control our children's futures we run the risk of becoming arrogant, prideful, and rebellious. We don't want to be a "hovercraft mother"—flying so low and so closely above our children's lives that we block their view of Jesus and hinder their ability to look to Him for answers instead of looking to us. Thankfully, Jochebed didn't hover over or hinder Moses from growing up to realize the One he should look to for help. Exercise your faith, friend. Step away from the scary waters God is asking you to leave your loved one in—and trust His plan:

> "For I know the plans I have for you," declares the Lord, "plans to prosper you and not to harm you, plans to give you hope and a future. Then you will call on me and come and pray to me, and I will listen to you. You will seek me and find me when you seek me with all your heart. I will be found by you," declares the Lord.
>
> Jeremiah 29:11–14 NIV

As you surrender your ideas of how the story should be written in the lives of those you love, you'll find sweet peace and rest for your soul.

When Jochebed followed the path leading up to the Nile, did she realize God was preparing a nation for newness of life? What looked like a curse at the time was God at work fulfilling His powerful plan.

Ask God, "What have you envisioned for my life, Father?" When you grasp the fullness of His plan, your own plans will be irrelevant. Today is not the day to draw back, or to remove what you courageously placed into God's keeping yesterday. God redeemed you to move, breathe, live, and love with courage that shakes the powers of darkness.

May God renew your courage and help you live inside of His blessing and protection. May you be led daily to His beautiful streams of living waters where your soul can be saved, refreshed, renewed, transformed. Remember, courage is measured by faith, and faith by courage. He sees ahead of you, and there's not one step He will ask you to take that He won't be right beside you. And if He asks you to give something over to Him, He'll give more back to you.

Step up to the water's edge, friend, courageously, with knees knocking. Remember: Courage helps us keep going, to surrender our all at the risk of losing it all. Because, in the end, we will gain it all.

Courage is the quality that enables a person to face difficulties, hardships, burdens, and not be consumed by fear. There's an inaudible voice I'm learning to listen to. And it is wonderfully powerful and full of wisdom and discernment; it fills me with courage at the appointed time, and makes me an overcomer when I might otherwise crumble in despair. When I begin to replace every defeating lie with the truth of who Jesus is, I find peace. How else can we have courage and remain faithful? Only with supernatural strength can we do supernatural things.

Take your place among the courageous leaders of old. Step up to lead by their example today, friend. And hopefully others will say of you, "I love that woman—she knows her God, and He knows her. I want some of that crocodile courage!"

COURAGE QUEST

1. What new information did you learn from Moses' mother, Jochebed?
2. What kind of courage would it take to place your child in a crocodile-infested river?
3. Consider the power of God in Jochebed's life. What miraculous things did God do to give Jochebed extra time with her baby boy?
4. In what areas of your life do you need to exercise "crocodile faith"?
5. Is there some circumstance or person God is calling you to relinquish control of?

11

Safe Haven

Was it the Shunammite woman's kind gestures that convinced the prophet Elisha to join her and her husband for a meal in their home as he traveled through Shunem?[1] Perhaps she leaned out the window of her house in her hospitable way, calling, "Come! Eat!"

We don't know what her posture was or the exact way she went about the invitation, but I envision her welcoming arms waving from her front door and beckoning to Elisha—as though drawing him from the dusty path below by an invisible cord. Into her safe haven, the place she held so dear: her home. And Elisha must have really felt at ease with her kind-hearted hospitality; this visit would not be his last.[2]

> "I'm certain," said the woman to her husband, "that this man who stops by with us all the time is a holy man of God. Why don't we add on a small room upstairs and furnish it with a

> bed and desk, chair and lamp, so that when he comes by he can stay with us?"
>
> 2 Kings 4:9–10 MESSAGE

Obviously, she was a detail girl! Neither her wealth nor her unanswered prayers for a child of her own had tainted her generous, hospitable spirit. With every movement, every gentle act of service, she focused on making sure Elisha was comfortable, instead of dwelling on the ache in her heart. Serving Elisha, the man who represented the power of God, was her first and most pleasurable priority. And as she prepared a room for him, little did she know she was making room for God to work in her life in amazing ways.

The dreamer in me wants to envision her rolling back the blankets, placing a delicious, freshly picked bowl of dates on Elisha's pillow. I see her papyrus reed welcome note positioned on his bedside table, next to the water cistern she'd carefully filled to the brim with refreshing spring water. Regardless of how her culture might have frowned upon her infertility, she would turn her heart toward home, filling her days with an others-minded approach to living. Serving others would prove to be the best way to occupy her childless arms.

If we think about our longest road trip and the exhaustion that came with it, we can imagine how much we'd appreciate having such a room prepared especially for us. "Ahhh . . . wonderful," we might murmur, falling into bed.

Right now, I'm stranded in an airport, heading home from Canada. I so look forward to my comfy bed. And as I write about the Shunammite woman, it's easy for me to visualize how incredible a room so thoughtfully arranged for me would feel at the end of this long day of delays and cancelled flights. But at least I'm not traveling by donkey, or on a camel in the intense desert heat, for miles on end as the wonder-working Elisha's life demanded. Imagine how truly grateful he must have been for the safe haven—a refuge from his exhausting journeys. What more could weary bones ask for? And as I sit here listening to the announcement of yet another delay, I want to make a reservation at the Shunammite Bed-and-Breakfast!

Courage Makes Room for God's Supernatural Power

I'm impressed, as I read about this courageous woman of the Bible, with how she chose to keep her heart centered on the good things of life instead of dwelling on the pain of her childless reality.

Where is our focus when life doesn't turn out the way we thought it would? Can we muster the courage to make room for God, and others, when our arms are empty and our dreams are dashed?

I remember a time when my dreams were dashed. I was a giddy bride-to-be with my whole life ahead of me. But the unexpected happened. During my premarital examination, my doctor discovered severe endometriosis, a medical condition that has the potential to cause infertility. The doctor explained that I needed to have a frank conversation with my fiancé. Fear and anxiety swept across my heart and I quickly went from elated to devastated. To think my lifelong dream of someday becoming a mother might *never happen.*

I remember the gut-wrenching conversation—the insecurity of telling the man I wanted to spend my life with that he might want to reconsider marrying me because the risks were high and the chances were slim that he'd ever have the pleasure of becoming a father. He assured me that his love was not contingent upon what I could give to him. Thankfully, modern medicine provided me with a surgical procedure, reversing the damage done by the endometrial growths that caused my infertility. By the next year I was able to give birth to our first child—a son.

When I think about how distracted I was during those uncertain days, how my pain turned my thoughts inward, I appreciate the Shunammite woman's story—how she focused on serving God using her childless arms and her empty nest. Perhaps you are in a season of life when you can't even focus on replacing the toilet paper roll. When to open yourself up to others in any way just hurts too much. It's okay, friend. There is a season for everything.[3] I am praying you will draw God in close, like the Shunammite drew Elisha in, as though by an invisible cord. Keep the lamp light on and allow the Light of the World to ease you, day by day as you welcome Him into the pain.

I think the Shunammite woman would comfort us. She, too, must have known the struggle against inward pain, wanting to fold her unfilled arms and give in to the same self-pity that so often wars against our beautiful spiritual freedom. She could have thought, *God doesn't care about me. Why should I do anything for Him?* Can you relate, friend? I can't tell you the number of times my own empty arms tried to put me in the corner emotionally. I really want to be transparent and tell the hard, cold truth here—that serving others wasn't on *my* radar either. But having the power of God inside of me helped me to heal and find rest.

We could say the reason the Shunammite woman was able to serve with such joy is because she was wealthy and would have had plenty to share. It's easy for us to assume the wealthy have no problems, isn't it? But it was because the Shunammite woman was wealthy that no one might ever have detected the lack burdening her generous heart. Thankfully, Elisha the prophet noticed. So the next time Elisha visited the Shunammite's home, he told his servant Gehazi to relay a very special message from his heart to hers:

> "You have gone to all this trouble for us; what can I do for you? Would you like to be mentioned to the king or to the captain of the army?" She answered, "I live among my own people [in peace and security and need no special favors]."
>
> 2 Kings 4:13 AMP

Was her response fueled by pride, humility, or surrender? It's hard to tell. But Elisha couldn't let her generosity go unrewarded. So he asked his servant Gehazi for suggestions on how to bless her for all she'd done for him. Gehazi remembered that the Shunammite woman had no children, and that her husband was old.

Elisha had been lavishly served and had been respected in her home. Although she had done these things without a personal agenda or expectations for something in return, Elisha wanted to do something for her. Well, Elisha eagerly sent word for her to come to him. Prophet Elisha's words must have felt like a song to her heart: "At this season next year, you will embrace a son."[4]

> She said, "No, my lord. O man of God, do not lie to your maidservant." But the woman conceived and gave birth to a son at that season the next year, just as Elisha had said to her.
>
> 2 Kings 4:16–17 AMP

Elisha wanted the Shunammite woman's dream to come true. And God would answer in a miraculous way, long after the contented Shunammite woman had resigned herself to serve God anyway. What about you? Have you resigned yourself to serve God—anyway? Trusting God with the result of your prayers?

Courage Prepares Us for Tomorrow

Elisha had spoken a prophetic word over her, and just as he had said, the Shunammite gave birth to a bouncing baby boy the following year! Yay! Bring out the cake, the bells and whistles, and the streamers! Oh, the unexpected joy she must have experienced! Her longtime dream of being a mother had been fulfilled.

Are some of you ladies reading this wanting to throw up about now? I bet you are! Because your prayers have gone unanswered? Please, keep reading, friend. . . .

One day after the child had grown up, he complained of a severe headache: "Oh, my head, my head!"[5] And just like that, tragedy strikes the Shunammite woman's life. Are you feeling guilty for being jealous a few minutes earlier because you thought the Shunammite woman got the happily ever after? Me too. But sometimes we aren't given the privilege of knowing our friends' whole stories.

Well, buckle up, friend. There's more. . . .

> The father said to his servant, "Carry him to his mother." And when he had lifted him and brought him to his mother, the child sat on her lap till noon, and then he died.
>
> 2 Kings 4:19–20

What? He died?

Yes. He died!

And the Shunammite woman "went up and laid him on the bed of the man of God and shut the door behind him and went out."[6] The safe haven she had created for Elisha was now the safe haven for her precious son's cold and lifeless body. And the Shunammite woman's arms were empty—again.

Talk about a diligent, courageous woman!

> She called to her husband and said, "Send me one of the servants and one of the donkeys, that I may quickly go to the man of God and come back again." And he said, "Why will you go to him today? It is neither new moon nor Sabbath." She said, *"All is well."*
>
> 2 Kings 4:22–24, emphasis added

All is well? Really? Imagine what your response would be. No doubt I'd be a royal mess! Panicking. Running in circles. Tweeting, Facebooking, and falling on the floor screaming: "Why, God, why?"

But I think the Shunammite woman gives us the courage to experience an unshaken confidence in God. Her testimony speaks for itself. Remember, even when her womb was barren and her arms empty, her heart was full of gratitude, pouring out blessings on Elisha, the man of God. And although she was grieved, her confident faith kept her calm in the face of tragedy and loss, and she was able to make clear-headed decisions. Do you have a confident faith, friend? Are you able to trust God with the dreams or relationships you called "dead"?

There was no time for chitchat or explanations. Her child was dead, and every ounce of her emotional and physical energies was focused on one thing—going to the man who could *do* something. The one who had the power to resurrect her lifeless dream—the child she so loved.

And to think all you and I have to do to make our request known to God is to bow our heads—right where we are—or look up into the blue sky and pray with eyes and hearts wide open, or envision Jesus sitting in the passenger seat beside us while in the carpool lane. Make your request known to God, friend.

The Shunammite woman saddled the donkey and said to her servant, "Drive [the animal] fast; do not slow down the pace for me unless I tell you."[7] She was one tough chick, emotionally, physically, and spiritually too! And with determination in her heart and faith in her steps, she set out to go meet Elisha in Mount Carmel. He was God's representative, the power of heaven, and she would go audaciously.

> When the man of God saw her at a distance, he said to Gehazi his servant, "Look, there is the Shunammite woman. Please run now to meet her and ask her, *'Is it well with you? Is it well with your husband? Is it well with the child?'*" And she answered, *"It is well."*
>
> 2 Kings 4:25–26 AMP, emphasis added

It is well? Are you kidding me? Lady, your child is dead, locked in the rooftop bedroom, and your response is "It is well"?

Imagine having such confidence that everything is going to be okay. Elisha was her safe haven—a refuge, her security. Elisha, the man of God who represented her Lord, was her "all is well." It was her Lord who had filled her with the confidence to serve Elisha through some of the darkest days of her life. And it was the Lord who had reshaped her shattered heart, filling her life with acts of service and sweet hospitality when her wanting arms were empty of children. It was her faith in God that enabled her, in times past, to think, live, act, and react. And now it was the Lord helping her remain steady in the overwhelming, painful loss of her child.

How else can we explain such courage? How else could she hold up underneath the weight of such grueling loss? It must have seemed unimaginable to have had her promise fulfilled—then taken away. We'd be plain mad! We'd want to shake our fist in the air and ask, "God, is this some kind of bad joke?" But we see the Shunammite woman's humility as she approaches Elisha, the man of God:

> And when she came to the mountain to the man of God, she caught hold of his feet. And Gehazi came to push her away. But the man of God said, "Leave her alone, for she is in bitter distress, and the Lord has hidden it from me and has not told me."
>
> 2 Kings 4:27

The Shunammite woman reminds Elisha how satisfied and content her life had been: "Did I ask my lord for a son? Did I not say, 'Do not deceive me?'"[8]

Have you ever felt God deceived you? Like you've been the victim of a very poor joke? You want to believe the promises of God but your unanswered prayers weigh heavy on your heart? Perhaps you fear exercising faith because if you get your hopes up and nothing happens, then what? Friend, God still has His pen in hand and He is writing a good story across the pages of your life. He is in the *process* of answering your prayers and He's not finished yet.

And Elisha, the man of God, wasn't finished either.

> He said to Gehazi, "Tie up your garment and take my staff in your hand and go. If you meet anyone, do not greet him, and if anyone greets you, do not reply."
>
> 2 Kings 4:29

But the Shunammite woman turns to Elisha and says, "As the Lord lives and as you yourself live, I will not leave you."[9] Smart girl! This was her best decision yet. And it's our best decision to not leave the presence of God, either. Can we find the courage to cling to Him? To trust in the Lord with all our heart? And never rely on what we think we know, like the Shunammite woman?

Help us, Lord, to remember that you are in everything and will show us the way to resolve all of our problems.[10] *Thank you for being our safe haven.*

The Shunammite woman had discerned Elisha's holiness the first time he stayed in her home, and his godly presence was the reason she'd made him a room in the highest point of her house. Elisha had a double portion of God's spirit, because he'd asked for it before God took the prophet Elijah to heaven.[11] The power of God in a single portion was powerful beyond words. But imagine having a double portion of God's spirit. This power at work in the Shunammite woman's life was the reason she could confidently say, "All is well." Even while her dead dream lay on her lap, her heart recognized the power source that would change her sad situation. And no one else—not even Gehazi, Elisha's servant—would do!

> So he arose and followed her. Gehazi went on ahead and laid the staff on the face of the child, but there was no sound or sign of life. Therefore he returned to meet him and told him, "The child has not awakened." When Elisha came into the house, he saw the child lying dead on his bed. So he went in and shut the door behind the two of them and prayed to the Lord. Then he went up and lay on the child, putting his mouth on his mouth, his eyes on his eyes, and his hands on his hands. And as he stretched himself upon him, the flesh of the child became warm. Then he got up again and walked once back and forth in the house, and went up and stretched himself upon him. The child sneezed seven times, and the child opened his eyes. Then he summoned Gehazi and said, "Call this Shunammite." So he called her. And when she came to him, he said, "Pick up your son." She came and fell at his feet, bowing to the ground. Then she picked up her son and went out.
>
> 2 Kings 4:30–37

The Shunammite woman had courageously stepped out of fear and acted with confidence—making room for God in her house, her heart, and her life in general. What about you? Where do you make room for God? Are you willing to step out of your fears? Please, don't allow yourself to live in a constant state of disappointment. Be like the Shunammite woman, who took her high hopes to Elisha for help.

Will you exercise your faith, believing that God can do what no one else can do? This is how we make room for God. This is where our confident faith comes from. This is what opens the way for God to work in miraculous ways in our lives too. Friend, sometimes we are afraid to live hopeful. But I think it's better to live with our faith launched sky-high—it keeps us looking up to the things hoped for. It's better to believe big than not at all.

Courage to Keep Trusting God

It takes courage to keep believing for good when bad things are happening all around us. And who sent us the false memo telling us that life would always be easy and every prayer we've prayed would be answered, and in the way we think best—if we'd only live for God? No wonder we struggle to live like the Shunammite woman, with full hearts, open homes, and strong arms to bless others. Friend, the blessings of God in our lives are not contingent upon any good we do, but on knowing how good Jesus *is*. As disappointment weaves its way into our lives, despair squelches our faith to believe that there will be brighter days. The Shunammite woman's life is a great example of what the power of God as the centerpiece for living can do.

So the big question of the day is: Can we trust God, even if our dreams have not been fulfilled? Can we press into our lives with an "It is well" faith, knowing that God is our safe haven? That He is a good God wanting what's best for us? Is it possible that the thing you called dead is not really dead at all, but a resurrection work in process—with God working behind the scenes of your life? This includes your dead marriage, your dead friendship, your health, finances, your child's dead faith, or any disappointments and confusions. I know it sounds cliché, but it's not—it's truth. The best truth I have to give to you, a truth that I believe is straight from God's heart to yours.

Want more courage, less fear? Then trust God with everything you are, and everything you have . . . no matter what. Trust Him when you don't understand and when you feel a little jealous because things seem to work out for other people. I think the Shunammite woman trusted God and she had peace, regardless of the pain and disappointment she experienced.

Who knew that one invitation to her home would make all the difference in the life of the Shunammite woman? And who knew one invitation would make all the difference in my life too?

When my nephew Matthew, who was in the 82nd Airborne, announced he would be stationed close to our home, we were thrilled. Soon Matthew became a regular guest, attending church services with us each week. My daughter and her kind husband prepared a room for Matthew, much like the rooftop room the Shunammite woman prepared for Elisha, with a bed, a table, a chair, and a lamp, so that when he came into town for a visit, he would have a comfortable place to stay. Matthew's life had been reshaped by the gospel. There was a marked difference in his demeanor. And more than anything, he wanted his military buddies to come to church with him. Each week, Matthew went forward, asking one of the pastoral team to pray for his buddies. But they never came, and Matthew was fatally hit by a vehicle while riding his motorcycle.

After the funeral services were over, the loss of Matthew left an empty space in our hearts. How we missed his visits.

I began to feel the nudge to extend an invitation to the guys Matthew lovingly referred to as brothers. And, as Elisha had accepted the Shunammite woman's invitation to come and eat in her home, five of Matthew's friends took us up on our invitation, coming back each week for church, food, and fellowship.

On the first visit, I found myself wishing for Matthew to be there with us, to see these beloved, prayed-for faces around our table. But then I realized that in some strange way—he was. It was Matthew's hospitable spirit, the way he cared for others with generous compassion, that had marked for the better the heart of every person sitting around our table. He was the reason we had gathered together in the first place. And I knew: We were witnessing heaven at work, because to make others feel truly at home with you is a powerful thing. To be a safe haven, to give others a sense of home—is there anything better in life? I think not, friend. And I think the Shunammite woman and Elisha would agree!

Matthew's prayers had been answered. Five of his buddies now attend church regularly, and we lovingly refer to them as our Sunday Soldiers. And they call me "Aunt LaTan." I didn't invite them with ulterior motives, any more than the Shunammite woman invited Elisha so that her prayers for a child would be answered. But I am thankful that God helped us use our empty arms and our empty nest for His service. And although Matthew can never be replaced, I'm humbled by how God gave me five other nephews to enjoy. I could have missed this blessing had I folded my arms, closed my heart, and blocked the door of my home. Matthew had been a home without walls—a safe haven. And now we get to do the same for a band of grieving soldiers who miss him.

The Shunammite woman makes me want to live hospitably. Hospitality can be hot dogs on paper plates or store-bought muffins and coffee. Ask God to help you to realize how to reach your full potential in creating a safe haven of rest in the middle of someone's very hard life. Don't disregard the power of the kind "hello" and warm smile you give to the girl behind the cash register. Or the homeless person you gave a ziplock bag of provisions to. Make room for God in your home, your heart, and in the most unlikely corridors of your life. He will amaze you with opportunities that are suited specifically for beautiful you. Only when we get to heaven will we realize the full extent of our simple kindnesses.

Will you make room for God when the daily grind and painful circumstances of life make you want to turn off your brilliant lamp light? Right in the middle of dashed dreams, unanswered prayers, inadequacies, fears, and insecurities? Like the Shunammite woman, while you are serving, your heart might long for so much more, but you will find true contentment by going for more of God. He will fill the deafening quiet spaces of your life with power and purpose. And no stand-in power, no fill-in healer, no secondary option will do, friend.

How could the Shunammite woman have known when she positioned the lamp in Elisha's room that the light of the world would soon restore a dream to her? And how can you and I possibly know all the future joys God has in mind for us? Friend, live confidently knowing God is busy restoring all you thought was lost forever. Jesus is your safe haven—your "all is well." Courage will come as you faithfully leave behind fear and insecurity for your wonderful new life of confidence and freedom!

When Jesus is near, all is well and
nothing seems difficult.
When he is absent, all is hard.

Thomas à Kempis[12]

COURAGE QUEST

1. How did the Shunammite woman's story inspire you to exercise hospitality?
2. Why do you think Elisha continued to visit the Shunammite woman's home? Do people want to come back to your home when they visit? Think about how we might set the stage to have people feel welcomed, loved, and cared for in our homes. This is a great way to display the love of God.
3. Is there something specific you have prayed for and God has not answered your prayers? How do you use your "empty arms" to courageously bless others while waiting for God to move?
4. How did courage help the Shunammite woman open her heart and her home, regardless of her heartache?
5. When her son died, no one but Elisha would do. She knew he had the power of God on his life and she went straight to him for help. Do you realize the power of God and go to Him with the dead and lifeless things in your life? Or do you try to work harder, wear yourself out trying to run to others, or sit alone pitying yourself?

12

Courage Coming

Journal Your Way Toward Courageous Living

Introduction

Dear Friend, I am so excited to offer a journal chapter where you can allow yourself to be open and vulnerable—writing your honest thoughts and feelings on each corresponding chapter page. I hope you feel the good changes inside of you as you relate to and perhaps even see a bit of yourself in each of the eleven women of the Bible I've written about. I cannot express to you how writing this book has changed me personally. These courageous women have become like best friends: guiding, teaching, and admonishing me toward courageous living. Their powerful stories have helped me to realize that my story also matters to God. And so does yours, friend.

I wish we could sit together for hours, recounting how the power of God's holy Word has replaced our fears and insecurities for a life of confidence and freedom. Wouldn't that be awesome? But for now, this journal section is intended for your eyes only. I pray you will spill your inner thoughts onto the pages offered here, finding satisfaction for every need hidden away inside your beautiful heart.

I had no idea of the extent of my personal need for courage until I began writing this book. As I opened my heart to receive all the wisdom these women offered, I saw courage coming, and fear and insecurity leaving. I truly sense a newfound confidence and freedom—greater than I have personally ever experienced before. And I can't wait for you to journal about your own courage experience. How blessed we are to come to Jesus, time and time again, as life tries to rob us of our courage.

So write the visions of your heart, friend, and come alive as you experience your newfound freedom by putting courage into action in your everyday circumstances!

Introduction

How or where do I currently lack courage? How do I struggle with fear, insecurities, intimidation, or a general lack of confidence? Honest confession is the first step toward powerful living. But it takes courage to confess our weaknesses. Give careful thought to what you write below and get ready for better tomorrows as you transparently confess.

I will confess here:

Chapter 1: Man Up and Lead!

Am I a Deborah, willing to courageously lead—no matter what? Or am I like Barak, afraid to step out and lead because I see myself as *less* powerful, *less* important, and *less* equipped than others?

Chapter 2: Messy Courage

In what areas of my life do I need healing? What do I need to courageously bring to God? I will write about what hinders my coming to Jesus here:

Chapter 3: Courage Comes in the Most Unlikely and Least Affluent

What do I have to offer God? Am I tightfisted or generous with *all* I have been entrusted with? Do I live closed-handedly or open-handedly?

Chapter 4: What's in Your Hand?

What is in my hand that God wants me to use for His glory? What keeps me from using the gifts God has given me? Fear? Insecurity? Voices from my past that have crippled my confidence?

Chapter 5: Own Your Tomorrows

How do I deal with the angry Nabals in my life? Am *I* an angry Nabal? How do I respond to others in need? When I can't control the poor behavior of others, how can I bring blessings to my family, as Abigail did?

Chapter 6: Enough

Do I feel I'm not enough? How have I allowed the enemy (Satan) to objectify me? Do I have a victim mentality or a victor mentality—knowing that God has redeemed my past and that what He has to say about me is better than anything others could think of me? Do I cling to His holy Word—the Bible—believing all that it says I am and all that it says Jesus is?

Is there something from my past hindering my future freedoms? I will write them here and let them go, knowing my King Jesus gazes upon me in love. Instead of taking *from* me, He *gave* every part of himself *for me*, on the cross, so that I can experience life to the fullest.

Chapter 7: Come Empty, Leave Full

What makes me feel empty inside? What do I thirst for more than Jesus? How often do I come to the well, asking for the Holy Spirit to fill me to overflowing with His refreshing streams of living water? Today, I choose life over death, and holy living over sin; I will write from my heart what I want my future well experience to be.

Chapter 8: Birthing Courage

I will write my own "Let it be to me as you have spoken." I place my whole life in your hands, knowing that for every fear, you will give abundant courage. I proclaim: you are my security and my confidence. Help me surrender my all to you so that I can birth courage in my life and experience true freedom, as you intended. Today, I write a new prayer of surrender:

Chapter 9: Naked Courage

With naked courage, I will bravely write a love letter to Jesus—the lover of my soul—baring myself fully and holding nothing back.

Chapter 10: Crocodile Faith

Is God asking me to place someone or something in the Nile River of my life? I will place a person, __________, or thing, __________, into God's safekeeping. I will trust God, knowing that He will position others, as He positioned Pharaoh's daughter, to fulfill His perfect end result.

Chapter 11: Safe Haven

Below I will write about circumstances I am currently facing that I need to bring to Jesus—my "All is well."

How can my life and my home be used by God as a safe haven, a place of refuge or rest?

Notes

Chapter 1: Man Up and Lead!

1. Judges 4:5. The palm tree was where the people came up for judgment.
2. Judges 4:6.
3. Romans 8:37. "No, in all these things we are more than conquerors, through him who loved us."
4. James 4:8 NIV. "Come near to God and he will come near to you."
5. Hebrews 12:1. "Therefore, since we are surrounded by so great a cloud of witnesses, let us also lay aside every weight, and sin which clings so closely, and let us run with endurance the race that is set before us."

Chapter 2: Messy Courage

1. Mark 5:25–28 NIV.
2. Mark 5:22 NIV. "Then, one of the synagogue leaders, Jairus, came, and when he saw Jesus, he fell at his feet."
3. Psalm 107:20 NIV. "He sent forth his word and healed them; he rescued them from the grave."
4. This Scripture puts into perspective just how unclean the woman truly was, after having experienced bleeding for twelve long years.
5. Unnamed pastor, heard in a sermon years ago at a church I was visiting.
6. Mark 5:26 NIV.
7. Anne Graham Lotz, *Just Give Me Jesus* (Nashville: W. Publishing Group, 2000), 182–183.

Chapter 3: Courage Comes in the Most Unlikely and Least Affluent

1. Mark 11:27–33. The authority of Jesus was challenged.
2. Philippians 4:19 NIV. "And my God will meet all your needs according to the riches of his glory in Christ Jesus."
3. Luke 16:13.

4. Luke 6:38 NIV. "Give, and it will be given to you. A good measure, pressed down, shaken together and running over, will be poured into your lap. For with the measure you use, it will be measured to you."

Chapter 4: What's in Your Hand?

1. Judges 5:21. This is part of the Song of Deborah, about the waters overcoming her enemy, Sisera.
2. Judges 4:9. "'Very well,' Deborah said, 'I will go with you. But because of the way you are going about this, the honor will not be yours, for the Lord will hand Sisera over to a woman.'"
3. 2 Peter 2:5 NIV. "If he did not spare the ancient world when he brought the flood on its ungodly people, but protected Noah, a preacher of righteousness, and seven others."
4. Exodus 14:21. "Then Moses stretched out his hand over the sea, and the Lord drove the sea back by a strong east wind all night and made the sea dry land."
5. Psalm 100:5 NIV. "For the Lord is good and his love endures forever; his faithfulness continues through all generations."
6. John 10:10 NIV. "The thief comes only to kill and steal and destroy; I have come that they may have life, and have it to the full."
7. Luke 1:37. "For nothing will be impossible with God."
8. Jeremiah 33:3 NIV. "Call to me and I will answer you and tell you great and unsearchable things you do not know."

Chapter 5: Own Your Tomorrows

1. 1 Samuel 25:22 NIV. "May God deal with David, be it ever so severely, if by morning I leave alive one male of all who belong to him!"
2. 1 Samuel 18:5 NIV. "Whatever mission Saul sent him on, David was so successful that Saul gave him a high rank in the army. This pleased all the troops, and Saul's officers as well."
3. 1 Samuel 25:3. "The woman was discerning and beautiful, but the man was harsh and badly behaved."
4. Galatians 3:13. "Christ redeemed us from the curse of the law by becoming a curse for us."
5. Psalm 139:5 NIV. "You hem me in, behind and before, and you lay your hand upon me."
6. Psalm 91:4 NIV. "He will cover you with his feathers, and under his wings you will find refuge; his faithfulness will be your shield and rampart."
7. 1 Samuel 25:20–22.
8. 1 Samuel 16:7. "Man looks on the outward appearance, but the Lord looks on the heart."
9. David Guzik, "1 Samuel 25—David, Nabal, and Abigail," https://enduringword.com/bible-commentary/1-samuel-25/.
10. 1 Samuel 25:36 NIV. "When Abigail went to Nabal, he was in the house holding a banquet like that of a king. He was in high spirits and very drunk. So she told him nothing at all until daybreak."
11. David Guzik, "1 Samuel 25—David, Nabal, and Abigail."

12. 1 Samuel 25:2 NIV. "A certain man in Maon, who had property there at Carmel, was very wealthy. He had a thousand goats and three thousand sheep, which he was shearing in Carmel."

13. Genesis 12:2. "I will make you into a great nation, and I will bless you and make your name great, so that you will be a blessing."

14. Proverbs 22:6 KJV. "Train up a child in the way he should go: and when he is old, he will not depart from it."

15. Matthew 21:5. "Behold, your king is coming to you, humble and mounted on a donkey, on a colt, the foal of a beast of burden."

Chapter 6: Enough

1. 2 Samuel 11:4 NIV. "(Now she was purifying herself from her monthly uncleanness.)"

2. 1 Samuel 17:42 NIV. "He looked David over and saw that he was little more than a boy, glowing with health and handsome, and he despised him."

3. Acts 13:22 NIV. "God testified concerning him: 'I have found David son of Jesse, a man after my own heart; he will do everything I want him to do.'"

4. Proverbs 16:27–29 TLB. "Idle hands are the devil's workshop; idle lips are his mouthpiece."

5. 2 Samuel 23:8–39. David's thirty chief warriors

6. Reference to Genesis 3, the fall of man.

7. 1 Samuel 17:36.

8. 1 Samuel 17:38–48.

9. 2 Samuel 11:26. "When the wife of Uriah heard that Uriah, her husband was dead, she lamented over her husband."

10. 2 Samuel 11:27. "And when the mourning was over, David sent and brought her to his house, and she became his wife and bore him a son."

11. 2 Samuel 12:19. "He is dead."

12. Kings 3:12. "Behold, I give you a wise and discerning mind, so that none like you has been before you and none like you shall arise after you."

13. Luke 8:17 NIV. "For there is nothing hidden that will not be disclosed, and nothing concealed that will not be known or brought out into the open."

14. Romans 5:8 NIV. "God demonstrates his own love for us in this: While we were still sinners, Christ died for us."

15. 1 Kings 4:29 NIV. "God gave Solomon wisdom and very great insight, and a breadth of understanding as measureless as the sand on the seashore."

16. Matthew 19:26 NIV. "With man this is impossible, but with God all things are possible."

17. Exodus 34:6. "The Lord passed before them and proclaimed, 'The Lord, the Lord, a God merciful and gracious, slow to anger, and abounding in steadfast love and faithfulness.'"

Chapter 7: Come Empty, Leave Full

1. Romans 1:29 NIV. "They have become filled with every kind of wickedness, evil, greed and depravity. They are full of envy, murder, strife, deceit and malice. They are gossips."

2. John 4:7.

3. Liz Curtis Higgs, "The Woman at the Well: Thirsty for Truth," *Today's Christian Woman* (July 2008), http://www.todayschristianwoman.com/articles/2008/july/woman-at-well.html.

4. "Woman of Samaria: The Woman Who Left Her Waterpot," https://www.biblegateway.com/resources/all-women-bible/Woman-Samaria.

5. Liz Curtis Higgs, "The Woman at the Well: Thirsty for Truth."

6. 1 John 1:9 NIV. "If we confess our sins, he is faithful and just and will forgive us our sins and purify us from all unrighteousness."

Chapter 8: Birthing Courage

1. Luke 1:28.

2. Reference to Deuteronomy 28:2–8.

3. Reference to promises made by God to His people for their obedience in Deuteronomy 28:12–13.

4. Matthew 1:18–23.

5. Luke 1:18 NIV.

6. Luke 1:19–20 NIV.

7. Philippians 1:6. "And I am certain of this, that he who began a good work in you will bring it to completion at the day of Jesus Christ."

Chapter 9: Naked Courage

1. Johnny Lee, vocal performance of "Lookin' For Love," by Bob Morrison, Patti Ryan, Wanda Mallette, Sony/ATV Music Publishing Group, originally released in 1980.

2. Genesis 3. The Fall.

3. Genesis 3:16 NIV. "Your desire will be for your husband."

4. Song of Solomon 3:1.

5. Song of Solomon 3:4.

6. Song of Solomon 1:16.

Chapter 10: Crocodile Faith

1. "The Nile River," www.thenilerivertas.weebly.com.

2. Genesis 41:40–45.

3. Genesis chapters 38–50 chronicle Joseph's life in Egypt.

4. John Dilworth, *Courage the Cowardly Dog*, 1999–2002, https://en.wikipedia.org/wiki/Courage_the_Cowardly_Dog.

Chapter 11: Safe Haven

1. 2 Kings 4:8 MESSAGE. "One day Elisha passed through Shunem. A leading lady of the town talked him into stopping for a meal."

2. 2 Kings 4:8 MESSAGE. "And then it became his custom: Whenever he passed through, he stopped by for a meal."

3. Ecclesiastes 3:1 NIV. "There is a time for everything, and a season for every activity under the heavens."

4. 2 Kings 4:16 AMP.

5. 2 Kings 4:18–19.

6. 2 Kings 4:21.

7. 2 Kings 4:24 AMP.

8. 2 Kings 4:28.

9. 2 Kings 4:30.

10. Proverbs 3:5–6 NIV. "Trust in the Lord with all your heart and lean not on your own understanding; in all your ways submit to him, and he will make your paths straight."

11. 2 Kings 2:9. "Please let there be a double portion of your spirit on me."

12. Thomas à Kempis, *The Imitation of Christ* (London: J.M. Dent & Sons, 1960), 61.

Acknowledgments

I am so thankful for the people in my life who have journeyed alongside me and believed in this book. Sometimes we need to reach out and touch a person with a Jesus-shaped heart—someone who will remind us that God is so much BIGGER than our fears and insecurities. A simple thank-you fails to convey my gratitude to each of you Jesus-shaped-heart friends. I'm grateful for each of you lovingly turning my face forward—toward *my* "better tomorrows."

To my husband, Joe, thank you for believing in me when I didn't believe in myself. Thank you for giving me courage to keep going, for keeping your thumb in my back, and for believing in the messages of my heart. I am so blessed to have you by my side as we strive toward courageous living together. You are the calm in my storm, the peace in my chaos. God knew exactly the kind of man best suited for my sometimes "undone" frazzled self.

To Kyle, Carolyn, Sparrow, Bryce, DaNae, Robbie, and baby bear on the way, being a mother, grandmother, and mother-in-law is the greatest platform I will ever stand on in this life—and the most treasured. You guys have taught me so much about courage and have helped me to live more courageously—although I often wonder where you came from, with your love for extreme sports. Thank you for loving the "chicken" in me anyway. Funny how I'm the one who seems to need the most courage in the family, and I'm writing a book *about* courage. Always remember, God will use *your* weaknesses too, to prove how strong and capable *He is*. I am blessed beyond words by your love.

To my parents and in-laws, thank you for being such great examples in life and love. My respect runs deep for each of you. Your life stories have inspired me and steadied my faith to keep going—courageously.

To my dear and precious friends (you know who you are). You guys are the ultimate prayer-warriors. Thank you for loving me so well, for cheering me along on my journey of becoming a courageous woman. You guys have courageously stood by me at weddings, bridal showers, baby showers, births, and deaths and, like Jesus, were the "lifters of my head" when life became overwhelming. I pray for God to amaze your lives with wonder. Thank you all for being a voice of reason, and sounding boards for me in mothering, in life, and in writing this book. What would I do without you?

To Blythe Daniel, the best agent in the world. I remember the day I met you. I knew you were a woman of integrity with a heart to see the God-dreams of others fulfilled. Your gentle approach helped me to stay the course when I really wanted to give up. You have a special way of bringing God's own heart to the table of life, and I feel truly humbled to have been given a chair next to yours—as one of your *many* authors. Your professionalism is unmatched. Thank you for your constant encouragement and faith in me. Thank you, Blythe!

To my friends and allies at Bethany House Publishers, who believed in the messages of this book and worked alongside me to bring a tool for courageous living to women everywhere, a simple thank-you doesn't convey my heartfelt gratitude. To Kim Bangs, I love your big toe! You saw the need for this book and courageously opened the way for a fear-driven world to have access. Once again, thank you all!

Live Courageously,
LaTan

LaTan Roland Murphy is an event speaker and vocalist whose passion and purpose is to encourage others. LaTan speaks with candid humility and raw honesty, drawing from her own experiences and real-life failures while inspiring audiences with hilarious personal stories. "God amazes me daily by honoring an ordinary girl like me to speak to extraordinary people," says LaTan, who loves inspiring others to look for everyday blessings in the middle of crazy-busy living. She also leads marriage seminars and enjoys helping singles discover their identity and confidence in Christ.

A Selah Award-nominated writer, LaTan has been a regularly featured columnist for the nationally recognized *WHOAwomen* magazine since its inception in 2010, with her articles presented through *WHOAwomen* on Fox News, *Inside Edition*, *The 700 Club*, and *The Daily Mail* in the UK. Her books have been highlighted in *Southern Writers* magazine as Must Reads. LaTan has also been published online at Girlfriends in God Devotional/Crosswalk.com; she is a columnist for Just 18 Summers, and has been featured on the American Daily Herald, Inspire a Fire, and Southern Ohio Christian Voice websites.

LaTan and her husband, Joe, who met when they were teenagers, celebrate thirty-four years of marriage and confess they are still growing up together. LaTan and Joe have three adult children, two sons, and a daughter. They are blessed to have a loving son-in-law and daughter-in-law "who feel more like biological children," and in her spare hours LaTan enjoys spending time with the granddaughter and grandson who totally captivate her heart. Visit her website at www.latanmurphy.com.